# A History

# Of The

# Brownsville Baptist Church

By

Arthur Ray Dixon

www.cockedhatpublishing.com

Copyright © 2018 Arthur Ray Dixon

All rights reserved.

ISBN-13: 978-1-946896-90-2

*"Finally, brothers, whatever is true,*
*Whatever is noble,*
*Whatever is right,*
*Whatever is pure,*
*Whatever is lovely,*
*Whatever is admirable,*
*Whatever is excellent or praiseworthy --*
*Think about such things.*

*Whatever you have learned or received or heard from me, or seen in me --*
*Put into practice.*
*And the God of peace will be with you."*

Philippians 4:8-9 (NIV)

# Foreword

## A word about the author:

Arthur Ray Dixon is one of the oldest continual members of the Brownsville Baptist Church joining in early 1945 as a ten year old. He remembers the great teachers present at the church in Mrs. Irene Crandall, Eugene Vaughn, Herbert Swindle, Jack Haines and Ed Thompson through his tenure at the church. During his senior year at Haywood High School, he answered the call to the gospel ministry as a bi-vocational preacher, because he felt the need of rural churches for a pastor. After a year at Union University, he was drafted into the military and spent twelve years in the active navy and reserves. He credited the naval reserves with financing his education by the summer cruises around the nation.

Returning from his active military assignment, he re-entered Union University and worked his way through the remaining four years by work at the University and from the military reserves. He set his sights for education and answered the call to the ministry whenever it was presented by the spirit of God.

Teaching a year at Bolivar Central High School, he returned to Haywood county to teach at Anderson Grammar School in the eighth grade. School and the work of the ministry seemed quite associated, and for the next thirty years, it allowed the author to obtain his college degrees and become active in his church work. He has preached the associational sermon, attended the Southern Baptist Convention as a delegate, and was a representative to the Baptist World Alliance in Stockholm, Sweden. In the course of his education he completed his B.S. at Union, his M.A. at the University of Memphis, his 45 hours above the masters and completed the work for his PhD in Education.

The author became interested in the history of his church, when he discovered that there was a lot of information about the families that contributed to the buildings, grounds and influences but all were based on an oral tradition from certain family members associated with those family names. This work is not attempting to discredit, disprove or challenge the oral traditions, but has investigated the claims and searched the minutes, local records and state archives to determine the extent of correctness in the claims. Some are exaggerated while others are dead center correct. Finding any kind of error makes a lot of questions arise as to the accuracy of any of the claims.

There has been some "tampering" with the evidences both in the church history records and in the county files with pencil markings, erasures and added notes that were not part of the original penmanship. These fallacies are discussed in the following pages.

The author owes appreciation to Mrs. Emma Nunn, Mrs. Melissa McKenzie, Miss Betty Goff, and the public librarian Mrs. E. Stephenson. A large thank you goes to our state "Baptist and Reflector" archive director in Nashville, who was instrumental in sending some very interesting facts that are included in this undertaking.

## Table of Contents

| | |
|---|---|
| Minister's Roll Call | 7 |
| Russell Springs Church - The Beginnings | 8 |
| Peter S. Gayle - Picking Up the Pieces | 11 |
| The Great Revival | 14 |
| The Bonds and the Owens | 15 |
| Spivey and Conner – Landmarkism | 16 |
| Thomas Owen and William Shelton - The Educators | 20 |
| Baptist United and Divided - After the War Years | 22 |
| First Baptist and Brownsville Baptist Split Amicably | 24 |
| Judge Bond and Ecumentalism Movement | 25 |
| The Land Swap and the Site of Today's Church | 26 |
| Brownsville Baptist Starts and Runs a College | 27 |
| Building with Province | 28 |
| Yellow Fever and the Building Program | 29 |
| A Labor of Love Becomes a Step in the Profession | 30 |
| Traditions and a Couple of Trees | 32 |
| Arrival of a Blazing Showman | 34 |
| Another Preacher Moves On to Higher Academic Pastures | 35 |
| Budget Problems and Calculations | 36 |
| The Era of the Qualified and Devoted Servants | 38 |
| Celebration of the First Hundred Years | 39 |
| The Present Sanctuary Rises | 40 |
| The Stained Glass Window Saga | 41 |
| The Howell Connection and the Mohler | 43 |
| Changing the Worship Experience | 45 |
| Short Sessions | 46 |
| The Youth Movement | 47 |
| Scholar Dr. Blake Westmoreland | 49 |
| H.K. Sorrell - A Lengthy Pastorate | 50 |
| The Current Connerley Era | 54 |
| Appendix | 61 |

# Ministers Of Brownsville Baptist Church
# 1825 to the Present

| | |
|---|---|
| Hosea Lanier | 1825 - ? |
| Peter S. Gale | 1837 -1845 |
| Thomas Owen (1) | 1845 -1848 |
| Aaron V. Spivey | 1848 -1852 |
| Champ C. Connor | 1852 -1854 |
| Thomas Owen (2) | 1854 -1856 |
| William Shelton | 1856 -1866 |
| William Henson Davis | 1866 |
| R. W. Norton | 1867 -1870 |
| L. R. Branham | 1870 |
| W. P. Bond | 1871 -1874 |
| G. W. Griffin | 1874 -1877 |
| S. M. Provence | 1878 -1880 |
| S. E. Gates | 1881 -1884 |
| C. S. Gardner | 1885 |
| L. P. Trotter | 1886 -1895 |
| Luther Little | 1896 -1898 |
| C. H. Anderson | 1898 -1902 |
| J. W. Lawrence | 1902 |
| J. N. Norris | 1904 -1906 |
| Gilbert Dobbs | 1908 -1911 |
| W. B. Hall | 1913 -1914 |
| E. L. Atwood | 1914 -1920 |
| M. C. Vick | 1920 -1921 |
| Wilson Woodcock | 1921 -1927 |
| N. M. Stigler | 1928 -1933 |
| A. S. Harwell | 1933 -1934 |
| L. L. Sedberry | 1934 -1937 |
| F. W. Roth | 1937 -1938 |
| L. A. Stephens | 1939 -1943 |
| R. L. Orr | 1944 -1950 |
| James Kelley | 1950 |
| Paul Harding | 1951 -1952 |
| James F. Yates | 1952 -1957 |
| Blake Westmoreland | 1957 -1958 |
| H. K. Sorrell | 1958-1988 |
| R. H. Connerley | 1989 - |

# Russell Springs Church- The Beginnings

With a weapon on his shoulder for protection from Indians and wild beasts, Bible-carrying Hosea Lanier traveled from Nutbush to clear flowing springs located approximately 1½ miles west of Brownsville on the land of John Russell to form the Russell Springs Baptist Church in 1825.

According to Goodspeed's *Early History of West Tennessee*, "The first Baptist ministers in the Haywood County vicinity were Revs. Hugh Coffee, Hosea Lanier, Obediah Dotson, Peter S. Gale, Robert Pulley, William R. Alexander, George W. Day and Champ C. Conner.[1] History indicates that at one time or another, all these men preached in the little wood building very similar to the one pictured above. For all practical and written proof, we conclude that Hosea Lanier was the first pastor of the congregation.

From the history of the "Church of God" in Chapter 26, *The History of the Churches Composing the Kehukee Association in 1885*, we found the following statement:

> *"Smithwick's Creek, Martin County.—This church was at first a branch of the one at Skewarkey. While in that condition the members met for worship at the residence of Brother Joshua Roberson, and had Elder Joseph Biggs to preach for them, and the church was eventually constituted in brother Roberson's House. About the year 1803 or 1804 the members built them a meeting-house on Hay's Branch, between two prongs of Smithwick's Creek, from which creek the church derived its name, and still requested Elder Biggs to serve them as pastor, which he consented to do, and served them as such until about the year 1820.*
>
> *Abraham Tice, a member of this church, exercised a ministerial gift, but was never ordained to the administration of gospel ordinances. Some years afterwards* **Hosea Lanier,** *a member of this church, after preaching several years, was ordained by Elders Joseph Biggs and Luke Ward; yet, notwithstanding the church requested it, he never gave his consent to take the pastoral care of her. He, however, served her in preaching and administering ordinances until about the year 1824 or 1825, when he took a letter of dismission from her and moved to the State of Tennessee, and settled on Hatchie River."*[2]

Hosea Franklin Lanier was born about 1762 to Benjamin Lanier and an unknown Kenan as the youngest of 5 boys in Tyrell District, North Carolina. His brothers were Jacob, Owen, Benjamin III, and Isham. He was married to Anna Ranier and came to Tennessee by way of Duplin County, North Carolina after her death. He later married Rachel Peal and apparently came to the area sometime in the very early 1820's. Hosea is

---

[1] Goodspeed, Early History of West Tennessee, *Early Haywood County Churches,* p. 828-829.
[2] Hassell, C. B. & Hassell, Sylvester, History of the Church of God, *History of the Churches of the Kuhukee Association,* 1886

listed as a 1st Corporal attached to the Third Regiment, Fifth Company of the Martin Regiment of the Muster Rolls of Soldier of the War of 1812, who were detached in 1814.[3] It is not definitely known as to his heirs or their histories although census records indicate his daughter Sallie Lanier born in 1820, married a J. A. Avery of Gibson County. It is known that in 2005, his great-great grand daughter, Sarah Goldsmith Maynard, was living in Milan as an 82 year old who was a source of good family information and is a direct descendant of Hosea Lanier.

As most settlers arrived by river travel, he most likely was a settler who came by way of the Mississippi River by way of the Hatchie River into Tipton County to the Russell Springs location.[4]

Little is known of the reception given at the Russell's Spring Church, however, we know that Hosea did return in his later days to North Carolina and is buried in Duplin County Cemetery.[5]

The Original Site . . . The Rev. H. K. Sorrell, pastor of Brownsville Baptist Church, points to the pond on the C. T. Hooper farm on Ripley highway that was known as Russell Springs, the site of the first Baptist Church in this County. The church will celebrate its Sesquicentennial during the period of Aug. 20-24. Members of this committee are shown with the Rev. Mr. Sorrell. They are (l. to r.) - Mrs. Werner W. Crandell, Joe Gibbs, Eugene Vaughan, chairman; John Gorman, Mrs. James Parker, Mrs. James C. Nunn, Allen Watts, and Mrs. Sorrell.

The site for Haywood County's first Baptist church was chosen next to the clear springs, which provided an excellent spot for baptism of converts. According to the Thomas history of Brownsville Baptist Church, the land chosen for this church belonged in 1929 to Arthur Smith. This site in 2009 was presently located in the southwest corner of Preston Place subdivision near a small pond that is presently visible in 2009 from State Highway 19. There are two large oaks present at the site which are over 100 years old and could mark the spot of the first building. The reason this site was chosen by Bro. Lanier for the church was *"due to the large spring of clear water, sufficient to admit the construction of a pool for baptism."*[6] The description of the church given by S. F. Thomas's father was that the surroundings of that large, plain, commodious building were large, grand old oaks in front of a large, clear-water spring.[7] In 2009, the small lake that sits on the site is continuously fed by springs. The waters from these springs fed a larger lake called Bomer Lake, which has subsequently been drained and houses built on the site.

---

[3] **The Militia of North Carolina 1812-1814**, published under declaration of the General Assembly of January 1871 by Stone and Uzzell, State Pritners and Binders. 1873.
[4] Duplin County Notes and Events, Duplin County Genealogical Society, Goldsboro, NC.
[5] ftp.rootsweb.com/pub/usgenweb/ nc/duplin/cemeteries/laniercem.txt
[6] Spencer F. Thomas. History of the Brownsville Baptist Church. Vol. 1. Minutes of the Brownsville Baptist Church. 1923. Appendix 2.
[7] Thomas. Op. cit. p 1.

The church did not have regular Sunday services, and met usually on the last Sunday of the month. This was common occurrence during early West Tennessee history with many ministers "riding a circuit" to serve widely separated churches in several locations. Members often met for Bible study in what is commonly referred to as Sunday school in present day churches.

Brownsville Baptist was probably one, if not the actual first church in Haywood County or Brownsville community as its date of origin corresponds with the establishment of Brownsville as a community. According to S. F. Thomas, the church was the first church founded in Haywood County. Other histories, including the Goodspeed history of this period dispute this claim, but conclusions of Goodspeed were questioned by families of members of the Brownsville Baptist Church.[8]

Shortly after the founding of the church, Russell Springs Baptist Church became one of the founding members of the Big Hatchie Baptist Association in 1828.

In the early 1830's, the church encountered a major theological controversy over the issue of support for foreign missions. Early settlers came to this area from Virginia and North Carolina just preceding and following the settlement of the Indian Issue by President Andrew Jackson with the storied "Indian Removal Act of 1824." Indian problems persisted in the area for several years, which made settlement difficult and dangerous. Mr. L. M. Short wrote a history of the church and according to this report, ***"The members of Russell Springs Church were among the early settlers of West Tennessee. Many had come from Virginia and North Carolina and were wealthy and educated. Brownsville and Haywood County have always been known as a moral and religious community while other counties in West Tennessee that were settled by men of infidel and agnostic ideas are still some what under that blighting influence."***[9] Although this reference might seem strong in today's theological terminology, in earlier days men who had professed no religious affiliation were often considered infidels or agnostic.

As a result of this "upbringing and evangelical leadership and because Luther Rice, the famous missionary to India, had converted many of Russell Spring's members in Virginia and North Carolina the issue of supporting missions was decided rather strongly in favor of missions.

Events of the ensuing years from 1824 to 1837 were difficult to historically reconstruct, since no written records exist from church minutes. Some letters and writings from people of the time and era give some indication to the events and occurrences that happened during that time. According to a September 8, 1952, article in the Memphis newspaper, ***The Commercial Appeal,*** the county was host to only one settled minister, who was the Rev. Ruben Alfin, who built a log cabin and conducted worship services in the town each Sabbath.[10] Rev. Alfin was not associated with Baptists, and records indicated that the Russell Springs Church did not have regularly scheduled services during this period and met infrequently on the fourth or last Sunday of the month. Thereby, the records from this era may not consider the church as being regular in attendance. Apparently, from all present records, the pastor from 1824 until 1837 was the "Bible toting-gun carrying Hosea Lanier," who rode his faithful steed from Nutbush to conduct services near the clear spring.

---

[8] Brownsville Haywood County Historical Society. ***History of Haywood County Tennessee, 1989. Walsworth Publishing, Marceline, MO. Don Mills, Inc. Salem WV. 1989. p. 260.***

[9] L. M. Short. ***A History of the Brownsville Baptist Church 1907.*** Appendix to Church Minutes Vol. 2 Brownsville Baptist Church.

[10] ***The Commercial Appeal,*** September 8, 1952, Scripps-Howard Publications, Memphis, Tennessee p.9

# Peter S. Gale - Picking Up the Pieces

In 1837, Rev. Peter S. Gale became pastor of the church and remained pastor for seven years. He was instrumental in the organization of the West Tennessee Baptist Convention and became its first president. The West Tennessee Baptist Convention was an organization of churches throughout the West Tennessee area and held an annual meeting to discuss problems and missions, and to examine the need for establishment of new churches in the area. The primary emphasis according to the Tennessee Baptist Convention records was in the field of evangelism. Initially, West Tennessee Baptists were a diversified group composed of "colored, white, and Indian." The balcony of the early church provided a place where the "colored" servants could attend services with the land-owners.[11]

Bro. Gayle was instrumental in the founding of the first black congregation in Nashville as the First Baptist Church in 1820's. He found no problem with preaching the gospel to any of his brothers and sisters, be they black, white or Indian in statue.

A synopsis of Peter Smith Gayle was found in the Biographical Sketches of Tennessee Ministers 1888, pages 166 to 169. Since he was indicative of the fine stock of ministers called to lead this church, this synopsis is quoted as follows:

*Peter Smith Gayle was born in Charlotte County, Va., May 20, 1802; was married to Mary M. Pettus, March 27, 1823; and was baptized in his native county of Charlotte some time before his marriage, perhaps by Elder Abner Clopton. He moved to Tennessee in 1826, settling in Giles County, and was shortly afterwards ordained to the ministry. In the early thirties (about '31 to '33) he was a pioneer minister and pastor in Nashville, predecessor of Dr. R. B. C. Howell, in the pastorate of the First Baptist Church. The church had suffered from the inroads of Campbellism, having lost the larger part of its membership and its house of worship. Elder Gayle rallied and banded together the faithful and elect few (some seven or eight) and built up the church to a membership of something like forty, and turned the work over to other hands. In 1836 he moved to Haywood County, in West Tennessee, taking charge of Russell Spring (now the Brownsville) Church. He was pastor of this and the Woodlawn Church, in the same county, for six or eight years, both of the churches prospering under his administration. In 1845 he moved to Denmark, Madison County, taking charge of the Jackson and Big Black (now Denmark) churches. In 1846 he became pastor of the First Church, Memphis, serving the church as pastor two years. The next three years he was pastor of Beale Street Church, a new interest just organized. He now moved to Madison County, Miss. and took charge of Mound Bluff and Clinton churches, serving them efficiently till his death, which occurred June 8, 1853, at the age of 51. At the time of his death he was holding a meeting with the Clinton Church with great success, the church having already received for baptism some seventy-five persons and he himself having baptized fourteen of the candidates the day before his death. He had been heard to say many times: "If it is the Lord's will for it to be so, I should like to die in the midst of a protracted meeting of great interest." So it was that his wish and prayer were answered. The*

---
[11] L. M. Short Op Cit. p.2.

*Clinton and Madison Masonic Lodges published very complimentary resolutions in regard to Elder Gayle, making mention of him as a "useful member of society, as a distinguished and devoted minister, and as having spent a handsome fortune in the service of his divine Master, in building churches, paying ministers, etc. "*

*Elder Gayle was one of the originators of the first State Convention, organized at Mill Creek Church, Davidson County, 1833, and was the first president of the West Tennessee Convention. He was in the organization of the first Baptist education society in West Tennessee, formed at Brownsville, July 26, 1835, and became the agent of the same. In the agitations and divisions of churches and associations in the thirties and forties, over mission and anti-mission, effort and anti-effort, questions, Elder Gayle was known as an "effort man," being a zealous advocate of missions and education, "performing more arduous labor and doing more for the Baptist cause, in the convention and throughout the state" than almost any other man." He was above medium size, somewhat stooped in his shoulders, of pleasing address, usually wearing a smile, especially while preaching. His whole soul seemed to be absorbed in his Master's business, but his smile and manner seemed to say, 'It is always pleasant to obey Jesus Christ." (J. H. B.)*

*In 1838 Elder Gayle was requested by the Big Hatchie Association to prepare a circular letter to be read before the body at the next annual meeting. The letter called forth a good deal of discussion and opposition, and was finally rejected. At that time there was considerable confusion, uncertainty and suspicion in the public mind. Campbellism was rife in many places, and Hyper-Calvinism (Hardshellism) everywhere. These were like Scylla and Charybdis, in avoiding one you were liable to make wreck on the other. So Elder Gayle, I take it, in seeking to refute the errors of his anti-mission brethren, was suspected by some of falling into the opposite error of Campbellism. The four propositions of his letter are interesting, whether we consider them entirely defensible or not: "First, that Jehovah intends to save sinners; second, that he works by means; third, that all the knowledge of man is received through the senses; fourth, that all the means used by God are exerted on man through the senses."*

*He defended his position from the charge of being Campbellite by saying that "Campbellism denies the doctrine of all Divine agency, other than that contained in the means alone, while his position declares God's truth and God's agency to be two things, the divine agency using and operating through the means (the Word of truth) to the accomplishment of the end, and without the Divine influence the means employed would never produce a single conversion." Living in an atmosphere of controversy, at a time when there was considerable excitement among Baptists over Boards, Conventions and Associations, Elder Gayle developed a penchant for polemical warfare, but his contention was always for Scriptural and New Testament practices.*

*In an article in The Baptist (August, 1838), on the subject of a proposed "General Association" for the State, he stoutly opposed such an organization as a substitute for the State Convention till they had thoroughly tried out the convention idea. He urged his "brethren to be firm and zealous in their efforts to build up the Tennessee Baptist Convention, just as it was, without addition or diminution, as to its construction; also to foster three other societies, as nearly on the same plan as the Convention as possible: A Tennessee Baptist Bible Society, a Tennessee Baptist Foreign Missionary Society Auxiliary to the Baptist Triennial Convention for Foreign Missions, and a Tennessee Baptist Education Society." But he advises to "move cautiously and to walk in the truth, and nothing but the truth"; and as to certain heretics who had given trouble to the Baptists he says, "it would be anything else to me, to say as little as possible on the subject, than a cheering hope and pleasing anticipation to be identified with them."*

*Benedict, in the revision of his great history (1845), had Elder Gayle as his correspondent for the Big Hatchie Association. The Baptists seem to be getting more solidly together and moving more united along Scriptural lines. Among other things in his communications it is gratifying to see this note of harmony and progress: "In 1844, at an extra meeting of the delegates from the churches of this and some of the neighboring Associations, the following questions were freely and fully discussed, and unanimously answered in the affirmative: '1. Ought each church to have her own bishop and deacons? 2. Ought the bishop to devote himself wholly to the duties of his office, and should the church sustain him in so doing? 3. Ought each church to assemble every Lord's day for public worship?' In ten years from 1835 there were added by baptism to this body upwards of twenty-four hundred members."*

*Elder Gayle had a fine family of eight children, two sons and six daughters. One of the daughters, Mrs. Fannie Gayle Job was a mother to the writer when as a boy-preacher he was supply pastor of the Central Church, Memphis, during the summer of 1880. Perhaps all the family are now are united on the "evergreen shore," where the voices of the glorified are tuned to "sing the song of Moses and the Lamb."* [12]

Bro. Gayle was indeed a great preacher and leader of his flocks wherever he roamed. He was one of the original founders of the First Baptist Church in Jackson. The First Baptist Church of Jackson was organized according to the articles of faith of that church on January 29, 1837, by Rev. John Finlay and Rev. Peter S. Gayle.[13]

---

[12] Burnett, J.J. *Sketches of Tennessee's Pioneer Baptist Preachers.* Nashville, Tenn.: Press of Marshall & Bruce Company, 1919. p. 166-169

[13] *The Goodspeed Publishing Co., History of Tennessee, 1886 History of Madison County*
Transcribed by David Donahue

# The Great Revival

In 1839, Russell Springs Baptist Church experienced a great revival, resulting in fifty-three people making professions of faith and being baptized in the Springs. Crowds grew to the point that opening the windows was necessary to seat those coming and allow for those stranded outside to hear the messenger. In inclement weather, it was said that pews were removed and the congregation stood shoulder to shoulder for hours to hear the gospel presented by a series of great preachers. Because of the large crowds attending Russell Springs Baptist Church, a cascade of prominent politicians of the day, with the likes of James K. Polk, Felix Grundy, and Davy Crockett, made their way to the pulpit to express their political opinions as well as their religious beliefs.

In 1841, a Temperance Society was organized, which cautioned members of the church to abstain from production, sale, and use of intoxicating liquors or face expulsion by the membership.

Researching the years from 1840 to 1850 has become difficult because of some altering of notes found in the church records by previous researchers, who opted to rewrite the notes changing names, striking through references and rewriting the notes in the margins on the note pages. Some of these factoids may or may not be accurate or rewritten to protect family traditions or previously learned oral traditions within the family block. Entire sections of records are absent or missing, which further raises some suspicions as to the accuracy of the recording or recorder. Therefore, further research from the Tennessee Baptist Convention is used to verify those facts concerning that period of the history of the church. Most of these mark outs involved the Bond family traditions. So, much of the traditional family references have to be viewed with some suspicions as to logic and reasoning behind the erasures.

# The Bonds and the Owens

By the spring of 1844, according to Mrs. Emma Nunn's notes, it became apparent that a new building was needed to accommodate the fast growing congregation of the Russell Springs Baptist Church. With a member, Thomas Bond, donating the land, the church began the construction of a new building at the corner of Washington and College Streets in Brownsville. With trustees Lynn S. Taliaferro, William Patton, and James Taylor assuming the building note, the building was constructed during the service of Rev. Thomas Owen and Rev. Aaron V. Spivey and was completed in 1848. Included in the deed for this church was the stipulation that *"the said church at Russell Springs do continue and remain an orderly Christian Assembly holding to and practicing the doctrine of immersion in water upon a profession of faith in Jesus Christ as the Son of God, and if it shall so happen that said church shall depart from and renounce said doctrine, or shall be dissolved by any cause whatever, then it shall be ... returned to the original land owners."* [14] These men and women of the founding church were "most decidedly Baptist" in belief and practice.

Bro. Thomas Owen was a distinctly different man from his contemporaries. He was born on September 10, 1792, in Henrico County, Virginia, as the tenth child of Matthew Hobson Owen and Judith Parsons. Having been taught morals and social graces by his mother, he developed an unwavering faith in God and made his public profession in 1824, after a short career in the law.

Bro. Owen at the young age of seventeen, taught school to in order to complete his education. A few years later he took up his residence in Richmond, Virginia in the office of clerk of the court, while studying law. Bro. Owen owes a change in his life to providence leading him to avoid going to the theater one evening when a disastrous fire took the lives of the Governor of Virginia and many prominent citizens of Richmond. He was invited to attend the program, but his firm adherence to his moral conviction to only attend the theater twice a month to avoid being distracted from the reality of life probably saved his life from the fire which engulfed the theater. He moved to Tennessee very shortly thereafter and became one of the original members of the Russell Springs congregation.

Elder Owen, as most men of God were called during this period, left for Haywood County, Tennessee, in 1831, after the Indian Removal Act of 1824. Soon after arriving in Brownsville, he was ordained and took an active role in the Russell Springs Church. He made concise statements like, "We are the elect because we are in Christ and not in Christ because we are the elect."[15] For more than half a century, he was a close student of the Bible and was particularly astute in the argument of doctrine and belief. His two terms of service to the church mark the only time that a pastor has left and returned to lead the body. Bro. Owen's death was in July, 1878, in Brownsville. A sermon collection of Thomas Owen's powerful oratory has been archived at the University of Bangor, located in Wales, England. A letter of inquiry to that facility was returned without comment on the sermon collection.

---

[14] Publication of Brownsville Baptist Church on Observance of 150th Anniversary 1975. p. 2.
[15] Borum. Op. Cit. p. 504.

# Spivey and Conner - Landmarkism

Pastor Aaron J. Spivey was born near Windsor, Bertie County, North Carolina, and was the youngest son of Elder Aaron Spivey and Margaret Spivey. He was educated at the University of North Carolina, where he graduated in 1830 during the founding days of that great institution. Bro. Spivey served on the first board of directors for Wake Forrest University and developed a great desire for university education. He joined his father's church after his profession of faith and moved to Haywood County, Tennessee, in 1835 or 1836, and settled what became known as Spivey Place, ten miles west of Brownsville on the Turnpike Road. He joined the Elim Baptist Church and was licensed and ordained by that church. He became the pastor of the Russell Springs Church and moved it to Brownsville, because he felt that the town had grown to a size where a church would be of more service near the court square area. His choice of plot was just two blocks north of the square. Collaborating with Thomas Bond, they chose the site on the corner of North Washington and College Streets.

L. M. Short's history of the church, a description of the location of the church was given:

> "Rev. A. J. Spivey succeeded Rev. Owen as pastor in 1848. That year the church moved into its new house of worship on Washington St., where the Crandall house now stands, and took the name of the Brownsville Baptist Church. The gallery was used for the Negroes to worship in."

The present site in 2017 is next to the home of the late local florist Tom Lea, according to county land records. With the moving of the Russell Springs Baptist Church congregation to the new church, the church soon changed its name to the Brownsville's First Baptist Church. Brother Spivey left the church and returned in 1850, to North Carolina to pastor the Cashier Baptist Church in Bertie, North Carolina. He was pastor there until his death, which occurred in 1855 or 1856, in the prime of a very useful life. His wife was Margaret T. Bond, who survived him a few years and left no children. [16]

In 1848, the West Tennessee Baptist Convention met in the newly constructed church with the great landmark Baptist, J. R. Graves, leading a very successful revival. The following is an account of this revival as reported in Biographies of Tennessee Baptist Ministers, on page 286.

> *As A REVIVALIST—In his early ministry, Doctor Graves held a number of protracted meetings, resulting in large additions to the churches where held. It was the writer's good fortune to be with him upon one of those occasions, at Brownsville, Tenn., 1849, when some seventy or eighty professions of religion were made by the best men and women of the place. His arguments, illustrations and appeals were of the highest order and the most pungent, he thought he ever heard, and had he have cultivated the revival talent, he could not have been excelled. One night during the revival referred to above, after a solemn appeal, he gave an opportunity for inquirers to come forward, and such a rush to the seats designated, he has never seen. Before he was thirty years old, over one thousand three hundred persons had professed religion in special meetings he held alone. This should be mentioned*

---

[16] Borum. Op. Cit. p. 586.

*to balance his controversial character. And in regard to his controversial penchant, he was always challenged, never the challenging party.*[17]

James Robertson Graves was an early exponent of the doctrine of landmarkism, which holds fast to the principle or idea that Baptists are separatist and should remain separatist in doctrine as well as practice. In essence, Graves promoted the idea that only Baptist could inherit eternal life if they believed in salvation by grace, baptism as evidence of that salvation and participation the *Lord's* Supper" were strictly enforced for Baptist only in the congregation. Graves rode horseback across West Tennessee preaching that salvation was only possible in a Baptist Church that practiced scriptural conversion, baptism and observance of the Lord's Supper. His "hellfire and damnation" sermons brought many churches to completely throw out non-Baptist theology, preachers and unfortunately some errant members. Because of his dramatic and dynamic presentation, many of his converts during this era of revival came forward because they had not met the conditions of the order and wanted to return to the landmarks of the Baptist belief.[18]

In 1850, Under Bro. Spivey's leadership, the Brownsville Baptist Church assisted in the organization and building of the Brownsville Female College. According to the Thomas history:

*In 1852 the Brownsville Female College was organized under the auspices of the West Tennessee Baptist Convention. The property now owned and*

*occupied by Haywood County High School, which at the time contained 37 acres, was purchased from Louis Jansen of Harleman County in consideration of the sum of $4,000. A good portion of the property was sold off and only about four acres left as school property. The property became home sites for families of Judge Bond, Mrs. Kate Williams, W. P. Adams, S. F. Thomas, J. O. Bomer, E. C. King, C. H. Berson and J. D. Anthony. Selling of these parcels amounted to approximately 30 acres. Some of the homes now occupying land on "College Hill date to these family fathers.*[19]

Baptistfemalecollege

Some sources argue this land for the school was donated and paid for by James Bond, and this argument is supported by a deed of trust for the land given to the school from Book L, page 232, in the County Registrar's Office. However, some county figures feel that the land sold to these families provided repayment to James

---
[17] Borum. Op. Cit. p. 283.
[18] Garrett, Jr., James Leo (2009) *Baptist Theology: A Four Century Study.* Mercer University Press. pp 213-216.
[19] Thomas. Op.Cit. p. 2

Bond. That issue is very undecided and remains questionable. Again we have to refer to some corrections or deletions found in the records by some researcher.

The sum paid for the church site on the corner of North Washington and College Streets was approximately $10,000, to organize and construct the building.[20] Apparently, there existed some disagreements in every sector when land ownership came into dispute at the church and school meetings. According to the church minutes, a portion of land was returned to members of the Bond family after construction of the church was completed when all of the land donated was not incorporated in the building of the new building in 1930.[21]

Under the leadership of the West Tennessee Baptist Convention, the school was renamed the West Tennessee Baptist Female College in 1852. For nearly 20 years, the convention supported the institution, which trained young women in the arts and social graces. L. M. Short said, **"For many years the school was the pride of the Baptists of the state of Tennessee."** [22]

In 1851, Rev. Champ C. Conner became pastor and began to schedule regular Sunday services. Many churches throughout West Tennessee knew the personable and exciting Champ Conner. Brother Conner was a champion of the idea that only Baptists had the right prescription for salvation and was often thought of in religious circles as being "Campbellite" in doctrine. Campbellites, which is considered a derogatory term by those of the movement were parts of a Christian movement that began on the American frontier during the Second Great Awakening in the early 1800's and continued with the dispute resulting in formation of the Churches of Christ. The principal arguments were for observance of the Lord's Supper on the first day of the week, every week and the submersion of believers for the remission of sin and salvation by maintaining the Christian life. Conner differed from this movement in that he preached salvation by grace alone, yet observance of the other two church ordinances as remembrances.[23]

*Champ Conner was a namesake in the early annals of Lauderdale County, Tennessee and we find the following in the Goodspeed Record on that county concerning his father and Champ C:*

*Capt. Champ C. Conner, a farmer and lumber dealer, of Lauderdale county, is a son of Champ C. and Ann E. (Slaughter) Conner, both natives of Virginia, the father born in 1811 and the mother in 1819. They married and lived in their native state until 1836 when they moved to Lauderdale County, then to Haywood County and then to Hernando, Mississippi. Two sons and four daughters were born to them. The father was an earnest and able minister, commencing when still a boy to labor in the Master's cause, and for over fifty years was actively engaged as minister in the Missionary Baptist Church, being a man of rare pulpit oratory and of fine ability, his attainments being the result of his own efforts and application For many years he was president of the Mississippi Female College at Hernando, Miss., at the same time continuing his ministerial work, and preaching often three sermons a day. After the college burned, he gave all of his time to his church work, and, after zealously working in this cause, died at the age of sixty-four, and in 1883, his faithful wife died. Capt. Conner, our subject is of Irish,*

---

[20] Deed Book L. Haywood County Registrar's Office, Brownsville, Tennessee. P. 232.
[21] Minutes of the Brownsville Baptist Church, 1932.
[22] Short Op. Cit. p.2.
[23] Garrett, Leroy. *The Stone-Campbell Movement: The Storey of the American Restoration Movement,* College Press, 2002 p.208

*English and Welsh descent, and the only surviving son; he was born April 21, 1841 in Lauderdale county; was educated at Madison College, at Brownsville, and the University of Mississippi. In 1861 he volunteered in a company of college boys, known as University Grays, and after the first battle of Manassas he was transferred to the Army of the West, raised Company K, Fourteenth Tennessee Cavalry, and was appointed captain, serving in that capacity until the close of the war, engaged in farming and merchandising, and in 1870 married Tillie Stephenson, and they have had four children: Hammett S., Champ C., Phillip B. and Hallie E. Capt. Conner is a Missionary Baptist; Mrs. Conner a Presbyterian. In politics he was an ardent Democrat. As a businessman he has been very successful. For thirty-five years he has been a resident of Lauderdale County. He is a man of fine social standing and business qualifications.*[i]

Joseph L. Borum, who was secretary of the Big Hatchie Association and a friend of Champ Conner, described him thusly:

*"Brother Conner possessed social qualities in a high degree; possessed a sprightly intellect; enjoyed a good joke; could join in a hearty laugh with his friends; was good at repartee; clear and forcible in an argument. He had a debate at one time with a Presiding Elder, in Gibson county, in which, I understood, he showed considerable skill as a logician and polemic. His piety increased with his years. It was very perceivable to me. The change was manifestly great."*[24]

Two years later and after considerable confusion, Rev. Conner left, and the church again called Rev. Thomas Owen, who served until 1856.

---

[24] Borum, Op. Cit. p.174

# Thomas Owen and William Shelton - Educators

William Shelton

Much of Rev. Owen's tenure was devoted to patching the relationships within the congregation of the family oriented body.

Rev. William Shelton *(pictured to the left)* assumed the pastor's position in 1856 and also served as the president of the West Tennessee Baptist Female College. He was born in Smith County, Tennessee on July 4, 1824 Rev. Shelton remained at Brownsville Baptist Church during the long Civil War years, where he became the father of five children. In the **"History of First Baptist Church, Murfreesboro"** it was learned that Bro. Shelton attended the University of Nashville and Madison University of New York. He was ordained in 1846 and became the pastor of Clarksville Baptist Church. He became professor of Greek and Theology at Union University of Murfreesboro, Tennessee. He returned to Murfreesboro after the time as president of the Brownsville Female College and taught Theology. In 1873, he became financial agent and professor of Moral and Intellectual Philosophy at the University of Nashville. The Shelton pastorate of ten years was the longest period of time that a minister had served at the church. "Few men were held in higher esteem or more beloved than Rev. William Shelton," said S. J. Thomas.[25] The church experienced a tremendous loss when Bro. Shelton left in 1866, to become president of Union University in Murfreesboro. After leaving Union University, Bro. Shelton served as President of Ewing College, Illinois. His last days were spent upon his retirement in Davidson County, Tennessee.

From the digital Library Kentuckiana we read:

*Dr. William Shelton was in his day one of the foremost ministers of the Baptist church in the South and one of its most prominent educators. He was at the head at different times of several leading educational institutions, and as a pastor and preacher and leader in his denomination was recognized as a man of power and a man of God. Dr. Shelton was born in Smith county, Tennessee, near Lebanon, July 4, 1824, making him 86 years of age at the time of his death. He was one of a large family, the only other survivor being his sister, Mrs. Martha Riddle, of Kansas City, Mo. Dr. Shelton graduated from the University at Nashville, and studied theology at Hamilton University, New York. He was successively pastor of the Baptist church at Clarksville Tenn., professor of Greek and Latin at the University of Murfreesboro, Tenn., president of Brownsville Female College, Tenn., and pastor of the Baptist church there, president of West Tennessee College at Jackson, Tenn., President of the University of Nashville, president of Ewing college, Ewing, Ill., president of Los Angeles University at Los Angeles California, president of Sweetwater Female College, Sweetwater, Tenn., and president of Stanford Female College here. He retired from active duty a number of*

---

[25] Thomas Op. Cit. p. 3

*years ago and has since made his home in this city with his daughter Mrs. J. C. McClary.*

*Dr. Shelton was married twice, his first wife being Miss Virginia Campbell, niece and adopted daughter of Gov. David Campbell of Virginia and sister of Gov. William Campbell of Tennessee. To this issue were born eight children two surviving Mrs. J. C. McClary, of this city, and Henry C. Shelton, of Seattle, Washington. He is survived by ten grandchildren among them being Dr. W. A. Shelton, a leading surgeon, of Kansas City, Miss Virginia Richeson, of Freeport, Ill., Miss Mary Richeson, of Gooding, Idaho, Richard Richeson, of Canada, Robert O. Saufley, of Parker, Arizona and Shelton M. Saufley, editor of the Interior Journal, of this city, and Margaret Milton, William and Elsie Shelton, of Seattle. He also leaves three great grandchildren. After the death of his first wife in 1867, Dr. Shelton was married to Mrs. Carrie W. Bass, of West Nashville, Tenn., who died in 1902, leaving no issue.*

*The degrees of L. L., D., Ph. D., and D. D. were conferred upon the deceased in early life by institutions in recognition of his signal ability and acknowledged leadership in the ministry and educational field.*[ii]

# Baptist United - Divided - After the War Years

Rev. W. H. Davis served out the duration of 1866, replacing Bro. Shelton. Because of Federal occupation, the black members of the church chose Bro. Davis to serve. During Bro. Davis's tenure and a short time thereafter, an interesting event occurred at the school. When the federal garrison occupying the South during and after the war prevented travel, the school endured several years of co-ed education as males were entered as students for the first and only time. Many feel that the school fell victim to Federal Reconstruction and was lost due to restrictions placed upon it by the Union Army's occupation. Many male students who were attending colleges elsewhere in the South could not travel due to the restrictions of the occupation forces, so they continued their education at the all female school. Late in 1866, being of mixed parentage, Rev. W. H. Davis resigned and left Tennessee for the friendlier confines of Texas. Bro. Davis became deeply involved in the Freedman's education movement or referred to as the carpetbagger movement. He rejected his Baptist roots and sought racial understanding through the United Methodist Church in Marshall, Texas as one of the founders and first president of Wiley University. Rev. Davis became a Methodist minister in Ohio. His epitaph revealed some of his life after leaving Texas and returning to Illinois. On October 18, 1898, Rev. and Mrs. Davis celebrated their golden Wedding at the home of Newton Davis. On that occasion the members of the family came together and in number were present who had witnessed the wedding. For a long period of years Rev. Mr. Davis has been a member of the Illinois Conference of the Methodist Church. Recently he was superannuated and the would occasionally supply various pulpits of several denominations. He was a fine old gentleman and was held in the highest esteem by the other ministers of the conference and by his many friends both in and out of the church. His death will be regretted by many. In his westward swing, Bro. Davis served as president of several colleges.

*Among the visionaries of that era were presidents revered in Wiley College history. Individuals who persevered in a climate of hostility in the South and in the face of great personal sacrifice were Wiley's first presidents:* **Rev. F. C. Moore (1873-1876)**, **Rev. W. H. Davis (1876-1885)**, **Rev. N. D. Clifford (1885-1888)**, **Rev. Dr. George Whitaker (1888-1889)**, *and* **Rev. Dr. P. A. Pool (1889-1893)**.[26]

After the Civil War, Rev. R. W. Norton became the pastor. In an era where the tension of slavery had existed prior to the war, the church in 1867 had a membership of 582 members with the majority membership at that time being ex-slaves. There was a spirit of harmony and understanding between the two races with services continuing unabated during this period of reconstruction. As a black brother indicated, "the master don't know no slaves or free, when it comes times to praise and worship God." One change occurred during this time as the large black gates used to barricade the balcony for the blacks flung open and the congregation mixed with family members sitting with ex-slaves or former house servants. Harmony was evident and enjoyed as both races worshiped together. However, feelings between races became more strained as more

---

[26] Lane, John J. *History of Education in Texas,* Government Printing Office, 1903, Washington, DC. p. 121.

carpetbaggers and scallywags invaded the area and fomented racial divides for their political purposes.[27]

During this time the pastor and members were forced to load the wagons and drive seven to eight miles to the Hatchie River to perform the ordinance of Baptism. Mr. Thomas remembers that during Bro. Norton's term, he joined with 25 other baptismal prospects on the banks of the Hatchie River for the baptismal service after a great revival by Dr. J. F. B. Mayes, who was pastor of First Baptist Church in Jackson.

Eventually, between the two congregations there developed changes in styles of worship. Despite the fact that during the war, Rev. Norton had been a confederate chaplain and fought for the institution of slavery, he pastured the flock as if there had been no separation or conflict between brethren. His preaching preached one Christ for all races.

However, as worship styles began to change, African-American brethren began to want to have their own style of worship services. Many voiced concerns that they would like a man of the cloth who understood their racial upbringing. Upon the resignation of Bro. Norton, Bro. Thomas Owen succeeded Rev. Norton and began to train black pastors to enter the ministry and lead their flock. Bro. Norton joined with a group of evangelists and headed for the Texas hill country of East Texas to spread the gospel there. His last pastorate was in the Texas community of Sherman, Texas.[28]

---

[27] **Op.cit. Thomas p. 87**
[28] ***The Marlin Democrat, Marlin, Texas, Thursday, March 31, 1904***

# First Baptist and Brownsville Baptist Split Amicably

So with the formation of the Southern Baptist Convention in South Carolina, members of the two congregations within the church chose to establish two separate churches due to differences in worship methods and along racial lines. According to both accounts, the separation was very cordial and due to differences in worship techniques and not for racial separation. Several black members remained among the one hundred and sixty members of the church that had opted to align with the newly founded Southern Baptist Convention.[29]

An interesting renaming of the churches into Brownsville Baptist Church and First Baptist Church occurred with the division of the two churches in the community. From the pages of ***The History of Haywood County, Tennessee 1989*** on page 254, the following account is reported:

> *It was the spirit of missionary zeal to bring the gospel to all men that prompted Brother Major Thomas Owen, pastor of the local white Baptist Church to assume the leadership of a black band of worshippers. In 1840, he opened the doors of the white church to a little band of two hundred blacks, which had been hidden in secret since 1830. Each Sunday they held service in the "white folks" church. This arrangement for worship continued for forty-five years.*
>
> *Brother Owen gave further assistance to the Black Baptist group by training Brother Martin Winfield in the ministry and saw that he was ordained. Brother Winfield held his first revival in 1866 in the Cumberland Presbyterian Church, the building of a white congregation. At the close of the revival, "The First Baptist Church" of Brownsville was organized with a thousand members. The first work of Brother Winfield as pastor was to get a church home for his congregation. A lot on Southeast corner at East College Street at Park Avenue was purchased and cleared. (In 1920, the church was sold for $5,000 and a new site on Jefferson Street was purchased to house the present building.)*[30]

With the splitting of the two congregations, the larger congregation of Black brethren in the body voted and chose the name First Baptist Church, and the remaining White congregation wishing to distinguish between the two churches, chose the name Brownsville Baptist Church.[31]

Arriving in Brownsville in 1870, the new pastor and president of the West Tennessee Female College was Rev. I. R. Branham. Rev. Branham was noted as being a man of wonderful culture and refinement as was his wife and family. They came from a very distinguished Georgia family, and his influence upon the students at the college was remarkable. Few men were ever so beloved as was Dr. Branham by those under him in school, or those who came in personal contact with him.[32]

---

[29] Short Op. Cit. p. 4
[30] ***History of Haywood County, Tennessee 1989***. Op. cite. p. 254.
[31] Short Op. Cit. p.5
[32] Short Op. Cit. p. 4

# Judge Bond and the Ecumenical Movement

During the trying days of the reconstruction era, Rev. Branham left the church, and moved to Macon, Georgia where he pastored the First Baptist Church of Macon. In an effort to find and maintain a pastor familiar with the community, the church called fellow church member Judge W. P. Bond (1871-1874) to become pastor of the church.

According to family members and the ***Bond Oral History***, Judge Bond was a noted Circuit Court Judge of wealth and influence in Tennessee affairs. The Judge gave up his law practice, was ordained, and became pastor of the church for three years. With Judge Bond as pastor, the church experienced many notable events including the famous Teasdale Revival with nearly 100 additions to the church and numerous officials in the community becoming active Baptist church members. Judge Bond along with several ladies of the congregation was instrumental in the organization of the Women's Missionary Society in 1872 with 15 members.[*]

Several church history documents indicated that some dissention from residual Landmarkists occurred with Judge Bond as pastor due to the church's open door policy with other religious faiths. According to these reports, many of the attendees of the church were also members of other church organizations in the city. Some political involvement was indicated in these documents, but not specifically stated due to the belief that diversity would create division and church conflict. A small section of the Landmarkists left the church and joined with surrounding sympathetic Landmarkist's churches. Judge Bond was deeply involved in the Reconstruction Era of Haywood County because he had, prior to the war, purchased large sums of gold and silver currencies from banks in the north. (Nunn, 2009) Since contracts were held strong by the court, he was allowed to keep his wealth, when others in the country were unable to enjoy their long labors in farming. It is thought by some sources that this wealth posed a problem in his tenure as pastor and resulted in his resignation and returning to the circuit judgeship that he held.

With the open door policy, by 1871, the membership increased dramatically, it became apparent to the church that their present sanctuary located on North Washington and the corner of West College Streets was not adequate to support the growing attendance. Also, due to the church building's proximity to the town center, various organizations were using the building for civic purposes. The congregation voted to sell the property in 1871 to the Masonic organization and build another sanctuary one block west of the town square at the corner of Wilson Street and West Main Street. This land also was partially donated by the Bond family as a sign of affection for Judge Bond.

---

[*] For further information on Judge Bond, please see the appendix article.

# The Land Swap and the Final Site of Today's Church

The site under donation involved a "swap" of pieces of land, as the political figures of the county were deeply invested in a railroad that was to run through Brownsville from Holly Springs, MS to Rutherford, TN. The site for the railroad station and loading platform was to be on the southwest corner of the property, which had been donated to the church. The Bond family instituted a "swap" by deeding the southeast corner of the plot to the church and then selling the southwest plot to the railroad stockholders. The swap appeared to be beneficial to both agencies.

While the new building was being designed, financed, and constructed, the body sold their building and continued to worship by meeting in the Haywood County Court House. Because of a depression and the effects of southern reconstruction, the church experienced a long eight-year wait before the building was completed in 1878. During this hard period for the church, Judge Bond and Rev. G. W. Griffin served from 1874 to 1878. With Judge Bond deeply involved in the church affairs, it was quite simple to obtain the court house gathering room for church services. His influence was quite prominent in the church business affairs and many church members became upset with his leadership. Yet, his years of leadership experienced phenomenal growth due to his interpretation and exposition of scripture.

According to the Emma Nunn history and letters of the Brownsville Baptist Church, Judge Bond was instrumental in organizing the Ladies Aid Society. According to Mrs. Nunn, this organization of ladies was instrumental in getting the finances to complete the building and also construct a parsonage for the pastor.

# Brownsville Baptists Start and Run College

When Rev. G. W. Griffin arrived in 1874, Brownsville Baptist Church assumed ownership of the West Tennessee Baptist Female College and held the property until about 1915. The eventual closing of the school came as a result of economic depression in the area around the turn of the century.

*This school was for many years the pride of the Baptists of the state, and few institutions in its day wielded so marked an influence over the womanhood of Tennessee, Mississippi, Arkansas, and Texas. Some of the most refined and cultured women of the South were attendants at this institution and many of the distinguished men of this day were the sons of these women and thus will its influence live for ages to come.*

*The earnest desire of the founders of this institution was the establishment of a great institution for women, and it was a sad moment to the descendants and successors when they had to give up the struggle for its existence and to close its doors for want of financial support to meet the demand for greater equipment. We are glad, however, that though it has passed from Baptist control under the wise judgment of the last board of trustees, it is still to be used for the improvement and development of the youth of our land, and while the dreams of its founders were not fully realized, still a wise Providence will see that their labors and dreams were not in vain. The property when sold to the county was with a provision in the deed that it should be used only for school purposes.*[33]

G. W. Griffin decided with the closing of the school that he would "go west, young man, to achieve his desire to work with young men and women in the wild western frontier. His first stop was at a Baptist congregation in Coalfield, Colorado. From there, he migrated up to Washington state. In the later years of his life, he returned to the west Tennessee area among his friends.

At the turn of the century, the church leased the school property to Professor F. R. Ogilvie for a Boys' Training School. This institution thrived for approximately eleven years. With the demise of this educational venture in 1911, eventually the school was sold to Haywood County for a public high school. Haywood County High School remained on the site until 1975, when the school was converted to a city and county museum. Today, this site continues to provide education by becoming an outstanding Lincoln museum, a Haywood County Museum and a site, which provides artistic, social, and recreational facilities through the Ann L. Marks Performing Center, facilities for Senior Citizens, a city park complex of ball fields and tennis courts, and the local branch of the Young Men's Christian Association for the community.

---

[33] Short. Op. Cit. p. 5

## Building with Province

In 1878, Rev. S. M. Province became pastor of the church. Owing to the fact that Rev. Province was an architect as well as a minister, his great work to the church consisted of completing the building process in October, 1878. The church underwent considerable trial during this construction phase. On more than one occasion, the building process stopped for various and sundry reasons. A great financial depression occurring during 1874 and loans and speculation on the bond money forced several stoppages. Shortly thereafter, a depreciation of property occurred and many loans that were taken against property of individuals in the church, were recalled by banks. Congress and the President of the United States acting to offset the national financial situation, depreciated money to halt the inflation in anticipation of the issuing of gold specie payment for all transactions. Since much of the money in the construction of the church was on promissory notes, the building committee labored intensively to make the payments necessary as construction proceeded at a snail's pace. Then, as a final note, once the building was completed, a yellow fever epidemic decimated the membership of the church in the late 1870's. An article in the March 31, 1875 issue of the **Brownsville Democrat,** it was reported that "The Baptist expect to hold services in the basement of their new church in a week or two."[34] Even the ceremonies celebrating the completion of the building had to be postponed almost a year until the mosquito-borne disease subsided.

The church took a decidedly active stand in treating those who fell victim to the fever. Under the leadership of the pastor, **The Howard Society** was formed to help victims of the Yellow Fever plague.

---

[34] **Brownsville Democrat.** "Local Briefs." Wednesday, March 31, 1875. p2
[iii] *Personal letter and notes*

# Yellow Fever Strikes Building Program

An interesting item of interest that happened in association with some of those who fell victim to the area wide epidemic of Yellow Fever and treated by the Howard Society. In 1989, the author received a genealogical request for assistance in locating a W. K. Linyard who was treated by the Howard Society medical group as he fell victim on the L & N Railroad train from Louisville toward Memphis. When conductors realized that there was a carrier of the fever aboard, they telegraphed the local railway depot and informed them that he had to be taken off the train. The Howard Society was called by the station keeper to assist with the very, very ill patient. Working desperately to save the gentleman was to no avail and he passed away on August 7, 1882 and was buried in the local Oakland cemetery. In the requested letter for information and a picture of the tombstone, it was discovered that Mr. Linyard was the piano player in the orchestra at the Ford Theater the night that President Abraham Lincoln was assassinated. It was on his "Steinway Baby Grand" that John Wilkes Booth fell breaking Booth's leg. It was Limyard that pointed to the escape tunnel under the stage where Booth escaped.[iii] The Howard Society functioned effectively until the end of the epidemic and lost about ten members due to the fever.

Finally, with the subsiding of the epidemic, the church dedicated in 1879 was finally officially opened in 1889 and, the church was formally dedicated at the meeting of the Tennessee State Baptist Convention, which met in the newly constructed $14,000 – $20,000 debt-free building. Several of the sources reporting the cost of the building differed, and it is thought, when the prices were quoted, they included furnishings, which would account for the different sums. Outstanding minister, Dr. T. G. Jones of the First Baptist Church of Nashville, preached the dedicatory sermon.

# A Labor of Love Becomes A Step In The Profession

In successive years, the church had a series of hardworking and dedicated pastors including:

| | | | |
|---|---|---|---|
| *S. E. Gates* | *1880* | *C. S. Gardner* | *1884* |
| *L. P. Trotter* | *1886-1895* | *Luther Little* | *1896-1898* |
| *C. H. Anderson* | *1898-1902* | *J. B. Lawrence* | *1902* |
| *J. N. Norris* | *1904* | *Gilbert Dobbs* | *1908-1911* |
| *W. B. Hall* | *1911-1914* | *E. L. Atwood* | *1914-1916* |
| *M. C. Vick* | *1916 – 1921.* | | |

Unfortunately, little of their service is known about some of these pastors. Among this group of men, several of the pastors made an impression upon the Tennessee and Southern Baptist communities. Two of these pastors left the church to assume positions of scholarship at Southern Baptist Theological Seminary in Louisville, Kentucky. One left the church to assume a position of leadership on a major Southern Baptist Convention Board. Others left the pulpit to achieve higher goals in the ministry at larger churches. Only one of these fine men left the pulpit for pursuits in the private sector.

Rev. E. C. Gates became pastor in 1880 and was described as one of the best orators of his generation. His sermons were preached with such intensity that the congregation was tremendously spell-bound during his orations. The Thomas History describes this preacher of the gospel in this manner:

> *In many respects Mr. Gates was the most remarkable preacher ever sent out by the denomination. His hold on the church and the denomination was so powerful that women stilled their children and men were fully awake. Although broken in health and with death looking him in the face, he came back to Tennessee from Texas after resigning the pastorate of the church here and took charge of the state mission work and brought about the great organization that has been such a power for good to the denomination in the state ever since.*[35]

Rev. Gates later left the state mission work here in Tennessee and returned to his native Texas at Pulaski, Texas and pastored the First Baptist Church there until his death.[36].

Rev. C. S. Gardner arrived at Brownsville Baptist upon the departure of beloved Rev. Gates in 1888. He remained only about one year, before leaving to assume the position of teacher at the Louisville Southern Baptist Theological Seminary. Bro. Gardner's tenure at Brownsville Baptist was noted by his scholarly and witty defenses of Baptist doctrine. At Louisville, he became one of the Southern Baptist Convention's great minds in Biblical interpretation and doctrine.

In one of the great debates of landmarkism vs. individual spiritualism, Rev. Gardner took the floor at the convention to present his seven basic points for the audience to consider. He said:

---

[35] Thomas Op. Cit. p. 5.
[36] Oswego Paladium Times, March 12, 1938, p. 7.

*"But, speaking generally, I think we will all agree that the Bible does not make known any philosophy of the plan of salvation. It is not a book of explanations; it is a revelation. It does not theorize; it declares. Its revelation consists of a body of great facts which are authoritatively published. Among these great facts we will agree that these are to be found:*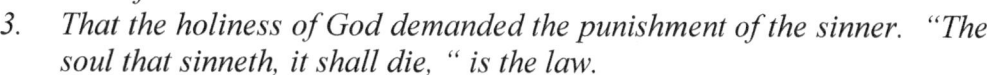
1. *That man is a condemned, and so far as his own power goes, a hopelessly condemned sinner.*
2. *That the movement for his salvation originated in the love of God.*
3. *That the holiness of God demanded the punishment of the sinner. "The soul that sinneth, it shall die, " is the law.*
4. *That God's eternal Son, by a mysterious incarnation, united himself with humanity.*
5. *That Christ took our guilt upon Himself and paid its penalty in His voluntary suffering and death.*
6. *That both the love and the holiness of God are expressed and satisfied in the voluntary and vicarious death of His incarnate Son.*
7. *That through faith in the Lord Jesus the sinner is justified and progressively sanctified, and at least is presented to God as a trophy of the cross" without spot or wrinkle, or any such thing."*

*If the Bible does not reveal these facts, it reveals nothing. They are only facts, and we do not find any synthesis of them in way of scientific explanation".*[37]

Rev. Gardner assumed one of the major roles in maintaining that Southern Baptist were glued to the scriptures as a basis for our belief and not into scientific theory of search for discovery.

Along with Rev. Province, Rev. Gardner's prowess for building led him to design and help construct numerous churches across the Southern Baptist Convention and beyond. The Delaware Street Missionary Baptist Church in Mobile, Alabama was the last church to receive his building and design abilities in 1899.[38] Interesting events occurred during Rev. L. P. Trotter's pastorate. The church organized the Women's Missionary Union and the Sunbeam Band. From the pages of Mississippi **Baptist Preachers** by L. S. Foster published in 1895, Bro. Trotter's father told him about a small town in Western Tennessee and the active Baptist Church there. His father was serving with the General Nathan Bedford Forrest Cavalry at the time he visited Brownsville. It was due to the General's love for the area that Bro. Trotter left the Southern Baptist Theological Seminary and came to the area. Bro. Trotter's wife was described as one of the loveliest women ever to grace the church. She was buried in Carrolton, MS at the Elim Methodist Church Cemetery by Bro. Trotter soon after he left Brownsville.

Bro. Trotter's hard work at the church also was emphasized in his labor to restore the Brownsville Female College back to its prosperous condition of the past. He appointed Professor P. H. Eager to serve as financial manager for the school, and Professor Eager reached churches all over the area and upgraded the school's materials and supplies.

---

[37] "Eleventh Annual Session of the Baptist Conference for Discussion of Current Questions." Baptist Congress Publishing. New York, 1894 p.52-56.
[38] History of the Delaware Street Missionary Baptist Church, website, 2008.

# Tradition and A Couple of Trees

Interesting events occurred during Rev. L. P. Trotter's pastorate. The church organized the Women's Missionary Union and the Sunbeam Band. From the pages of Mississippi *Baptist Preachers* by L. S. Foster published in 1895, Bro. Trotter's father told him about a small town in Western Tennessee and the active Baptist Church there. His father was serving with the General Nathan Bedford Forrest Cavalry at the time he visited Brownsville. It was due to the General's love for the area that Bro. Trotter left the Southern Baptist Theological Seminary and came to the area. Bro. Trotter's wife was described as one of the loveliest women ever to grace the church. She was buried in Carrolton, MS at the Elim Methodist Church Cemetery by Bro. Trotter soon after he left Brownsville.

An interesting item occurred during 1888 when special recognition was given to the church by the First Baptist Church in Covington recognizing the founding efforts of Reverend Major Thomas Owen, who founded the "mission" in Covington from the Brownsville Baptist Church. A ceremony including the joint congregations from the First Baptist Church in Covington and Brownsville Baptist planted a tree on the right side of the church front in Bro. Owens' memory. The planting commemorated on the date that the First Baptist Church in Covington was officially organized as a church from the Brownsville Baptist Church's mission started by Bro. Owens in Covington forty years earlier.[39] That tree grew through the concrete and asphalt in the parking area beside the church in the year 2000, resisting the attempts of many to cut the tree down to secure more parking spaces. However, with a strong stormy wind in 2005, the tree lost a large portion of its top, and for safety reasons was cut down and lost to the ages. A second tree, a large pecan tree was planted on the left by the joint congregations to cement the relationships between Brownsville Baptist members and the congregation of First Baptist Church in Covington. That pecan tree grew and towers above the church in 2017 and still produces a bounty crop of pecans annually.

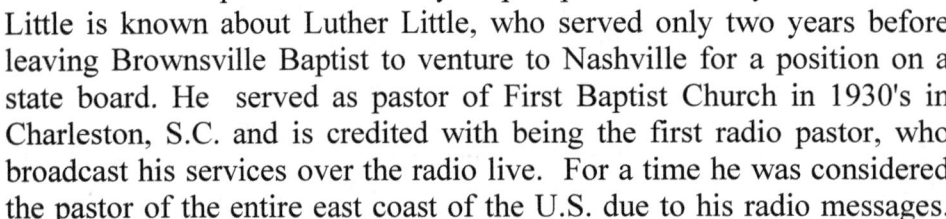
Luther Little

Little is known about Luther Little, who served only two years before leaving Brownsville Baptist to venture to Nashville for a position on a state board. He served as pastor of First Baptist Church in 1930's in Charleston, S.C. and is credited with being the first radio pastor, who broadcast his services over the radio live. For a time he was considered the pastor of the entire east coast of the U.S. due to his radio messages. His death and burial occurred in Jackson, Kentucky on February 10, 1945. Bro. Luther Little came to the church from Southern Baptist Theological Seminary and became a dynamic preacher of the gospel. According to L. M. Short's account, Bro. Little *".. was a magnetic speaker and universally loved man by his people."*[40]

Rev. Charles H. Anderson served from 1898 to 1902 and was recognized by both early church historians as a man of spiritual power and probing prayer. However in 1902, Brother Anderson became ill and left for the warm climate of New Mexico. Unfortunately, he passed away shortly after arriving in New Mexico in 1902.

Arriving on a train from Oklahoma, Rev. J. B. Lawrence answered the call to the church in 1902. Bro. Lawrence served only shortly and left Brownsville to become the secretary of the Southern Baptist Home Mission Board in 1902. Bro. Lawrence became famous in the early 1900's in Americus, GA by his insistence on humane treatment of Blacks in the pursuit of Justice. An article appears on page 12 of the Booker T.

---

[39] History of Haywood County, Tennessee 1989. Op. Cit. p. 264.
[40] Thomas. Op. Cit. p. 2.

Washington papers detailing how a mob was attempting to lynch a Black man who fought several whites when he was overwhelmed and beaten by a mob. He was shot and hauled away to jail and when Bro. Lawrence heard of the injustice, he and three other clergymen followed some of the parishioners of their churches into the jail to stop the lynching and subsequent burning of the man. He met the threat, "Preacher, get out of here or we're going to burn you, too." Bro. Lawrence had to be forcefully removed from the jail under threat of his life from the mob. He defended himself by saying, "Black or white, it is not right to legally or illegally lynch a man for a petty crime of which you accuse him." Bro. Lawrence was beaten by several of his own churchmen.[41] Needless to say, Bro. Lawrence left town rather quickly and quietly under fear for his life.

It was with the Lawrence report that slowly the membership of Brownsville Baptist reverted to a segregated congregation with many of the blacks deciding to join with the First Baptist Church. Some members felt that the separation was rather contemptuous while others felt that the worship styles favored by the different races was the actual culprit that led to the segregation of the body. None of this assumption appears in the church minutes, but the statistics indicate with the departure of Bro. Lawrence, there also departed the vast majority of the several hundred ex-slaves to other grounds.

The church met sporadically during 1903 and early 1904 while attempts were made to obtain a pastor. The services of J. N. Norris were secured in 1904 to serve the church. His tenure lasted only a short six months when Bro. Norris left the pulpit to become a successful lawyer in Western Tennessee. .

---

[41] The Booker T. Washington Papers, The University of Illinois Press. 1982. p. 243.-245.

## Arrival of A Blazing Showman

Leaving his pulpit in Paducah, Kentucky, Bro. Gilbert Dobbs stepped into the opening and served the church admirably for four years, before leaving to pastor another church in nearby Shelby County. Evidence that Brownsville Baptist Church was known across the land as a church that developed and trained great pastors was evident when the *History of Indiana Churches* recorded his arrival at Brownsville Baptist by saying: "Rev. Gilbert Dobbs is now pastor of one of the strongest churches in the south."[42]

Bro. Dobbs was known for his sermon antics and illustrations while preaching. Once in a church service he chose to challenge some age old traditions that had lessened the effect of seasonal observances of Easter and Christmas. So, he chose to deliver a sermon dressed as Santa Claus. During the service as he tore off portions of the suit to illustrate his points, he got too close to a candle near the pulpit and promptly burst into flames. Deacons rushed to his aid putting out the fire quickly, but unfortunately were unable to prevent some facial burns. The incident made the front page of the New York Times in New York City.[43] In 1904, Bro. Dobbs addressed the national convention of Baptists in St. Louis and preached the opening sermon on missions. He was well known across the south for his emphasis on winning souls. Bro. Dobbs left the pulpit in 1911.

---

[42] Stott, William D., Indiana Baptist History 1798-1908, Franklin College Press, Franklin, IN p.261.
[43] New York Times, December 26, 1909. p.1.

# Another Preacher Moves On To Higher Pastures

W. B. Hall came to Brownsville Baptist from Owingsville, Kentucky but served only a short four months, before he also left to assume the pastor's position at another church in Madison County. Bro. Hall was noted for his revision of the basic Hebrew Text Book for Spiritual Learners. He was noted for his intellectual sermons based on word studies found in Hebrew and Greek word meanings. He was often referred to the walking "original version" of the scriptures.[44]

The rapid movement of pastors during this period was atypical of the events of the early 1900's with rapid expansion and growth in the nation's industrial revolution. Many church members were leaving the countryside to move to the larger industrial areas for work. Many of the pastors found difficulty in finances as the smaller congregation of the church found some difficulty in properly reimbursing their leaders.

Some sources indicate that family problems had arisen within the congregation and that the church was struggling to resolve these issues. According to the Short History, family problems were pressuring the congregation and a power struggle over the leadership of the church was intensifying. In this problem era, small communities like Brownsville struggled to keep their institutions alive and functioning.

At this point in the history, a observational point must be undertaken. Throughout its history, the church has been troubled with "persons of authority" who assume a powerful role in conducting affairs of the body. Upon reading the notes from the church histories, church minutes and oral traditions, it was basically a problem back during the early 1900-1910 years to the point that it probably affected pastors and parishioners attending the services of the church. Stability returned with the arrival of Bro. E. L. Atwood. Bro. Atwood reached across arguments, denominational and family lines to pull together families and other congregations in the community. His preaching raised a public sentiment and spirit about morality and growth in the community, because he said, "You must reach out beyond your family and immediate friends, if you are going to continue to exist as a church." Reaching out, the church re-organized the Young Women's Auxilliary. Brother Atwood was especially powerful in his visitation program and became friends with many in the community regardless of religious affiliation. According to L. M. Short, ***"Few men were loved in the community as was Dr. Atwood."***[45]

DR. E. L. ATWOOD, President

Bro. Atwood left Brownsville and settled in St. Petersburg, Florida for his retirement years. The St. Petersburg Independent News report that he became ill and passed away in late September 1941 after more than 20 years in the pastorate. His epitaph reported ***"Here is one of the last great theologians with a big heart for all his neighbors regardless of their belief."***[46]

---

[44] Conversation with Mrs. Emma Ryals on March 4, 1974.
[45] Short. Op Cit. p. 5.
[46] St. Petersburg Evening Independent, September 29, 1941, p. 7.

# Budget Problems and Calculations

Church records indicate that the church budget in 1914 was $3,322.51, during Dr. Atwood's time as pastor with 82 church additions during 1914. It was the sale of the College Hill properties for $5,000 to Haywood County that provided the church with operating expenses for some of the year.

Indications from several of the handwritten histories and from the church minutes, hint that some sort of financial problem may have occurred during the latter years of Dr. Atwood's service and during the beginnings of Dr. M. C. Vicks' term. There was no reason evident from the records to indicate the nature of this problem, but the evidence is confusing as to the hesitation of the church to begin construction even though there were ample funds in the treasury to start construction on the proposed new building. Judging from the church minutes, there was considerable disagreement in the pros and cons on most issues with the same groups siding on the issues. Indications were that the family problems previously mentioned had resurfaced and affected the church's decision to continue the building program. Notes from the minutes written by Ben F. Clark indicate that some turmoil in the church has literally erased records during the 1914-1918 era. The following is a quote from the minutes of 1918:

> *An explanation for missing minutes*
> This church had contemplated building a new house of worship for several years and about two years ago gave a banquet and at that banquet and in other ways had raised about $40,000 in subscriptions, but before we could get under headway in building the country was plunged into the Great World War and conditions became so unsettled and building materials and labor so high that we postponed building for a time but the talk of building became so persistent that the deacons held a meeting to discuss means and plans either for a new house or repairing the old which plans were put before the church and it was decided to let Bro. R. W. Bond chairman of the building committee confer with the contractors as to the best terms and as to new house or repairing the old and report his findings to a business meeting of the church to be held at the morning service hour of Sunday, May 2/20. At this meeting Mr. L. M. Short, at his urgent request was removed from the building committee and Miss Sally Bond elected in his stead. The church met in conference per previous agreement, Bro. M. C. Vick in chair, to receive report from building committee, according to previous meeting – on which occasion Bro. R. W. Bond chairman of said committee reported as follows – Proposition repairing the old house by adding S. S. rooms in rear as to add auditorium in front later and proper repairs to old building would cost from $60,000 to $70,000, which proposition 2 which contemplated carrying out the original plan as to size, appearance, of original plan but embraced only the hull of the house that is the outside walls, roof, and basements were to be complete so the church could use it for worship would cost from $6,000 to $7,000. This second proposition was adopted and the chair asked to appoint a committee of 10 to solicit subscriptions –said subscriptions to be made in a shape that they would be bankable. Said committee to report their success on Sunday, May 9/20.[47]

---

[47] Minutes of the Brownsville Baptist Church, Vol. 2. p.76.

1879's Church

It is quite apparent that the skirting of the issue of missing funds was completely bypassed in the explanation. Apparently, the church had used approximately $30,000 of donated building funds in the operating budget, or other projects or salaries had "visited the treasury." However, there was no proof of any improper behavior or suspicious action, but there was enough tension among members of the committee that several opted to leave the group. The complaint centered on the collection of funds in a fund raising project that were used for another project, which was not lawful at the time. The result was that several businessmen and two lawyers left the congregation in dispute

# The Era of Qualified and Devoted Servants

In the 1920's, the church began a long series of qualified and devoted servants in:

| | |
|---|---|
| Wilson Woodcock | 1921 -1927 |
| N. M. Stigler | 1928 -1933 |
| A. S. Harwell | 1933 -1934 |
| L. S. Sedberry | 1934 -1937 |
| F. W. Roth | 1937 -1938 |
| L. A. Stephens | 1939 -1943 |

Realizing the questions floating among the congregation, members of the pulpit committed selected the former treasurer of the Tennessee Baptist Convention in Bro. Wilson Woodcock. Under his strong leadership Bro. Woodcock, the committee started a new financial drive and contributions reached $10,152 for a new building. Because the old Gothic styled church was leaking badly and in need of almost total reconstruction, the old church was torn down and the breaking of ground for a new Sunday school building occurred on May 1, 1923.

The Thomas history of the church points out the unity and spirit that abided in the church in spite of occasional disagreements – *"There have never been any serious dissentions, and no factions trying to be greatest or to control. It has always been like one devoted family. For all this we should thank God and take courage."* [48]

The church building committee was appointed and after considerable discussion the building committee of William Thomas, L. M. Short, Carey Lay, R. N. Bond, R. M. Chambliss, Miss Sally Bond, and Mrs. M. L. Davis was appointed. Considerable discussion arose when funding was insufficient to cover the cost of building the new auditorium and Sunday school space at the same time. Therefore, the committee voted to recommend to the church that a Sunday school facility be constructed first with the congregation to meet in the Sunday School Building until the auditorium could be completed. Opposition to this plan was voiced, and several members of the committee asked to be replaced.

Finally construction began and the Sunday School Building was constructed first at the cost of approximately $35,000. The church also prepared to build a new auditorium patterned after the original settings for the old College Street Church at the corner of College and Washington. Again the church met in the Haywood County Court House until the building was completed.

Finally, on Sunday morning, February 24, 1924, members moved the Church from the Court House into the presently occupied three-storied Sunday School Building. On November 1, 1925 nearly a year later, the church formally dedicated the building. During the dedicatory services, Dr. P. E. Burroughs preached the morning service, and Dr. W. D. Hudgins preached the evening message in an all-day service at the church. .

---

[48] Thomas Op. Cit. p. 4.

# Celebration of First One Hundred Years

The church celebrated its first one hundred years of existence by a week of services and events that followed. During this week of celebration, former pastors, Dr. E. L. Atwood and Rev. M. C. Vick returned to preach inspiring messages. Southern Baptist Convention ministers like Dr. Van Ness, Dr. J. D. Freeman, and Dr. A. U. Boone brought messages the other evenings of the week, and the church announced the formation of a Girls' Auxilliary and the Royal Ambassadors. The events of the week culminated with a banquet given by the ladies of the church, and over 300 members of the church family were present.

In late 1927, the church was instrumental in organizing the Big Hatchie Laymen, which later became the brotherhood of Big Hatchie Churches. However, it was on June 15, 1959, over thirty years later, that Brownsville Baptist Church officially organized the Baptist Brotherhood in the church.

In 1927, Bro. Wilson Woodcock resigned as pastor to accept the pulpit of the College Park Church in Greensboro, North Carolina. He remained pastor there until 1948, when he retired as reported in the Greensboro News on November 29, 1948. In later editions of the Greensboro News, Bro. Woodcock was still busy organizing and leading movements to better the community of Greensboro. Quoted below is a report by Robert Farley on March 13th edition of the 1993 Greensboro News:

*Posted: Saturday, March 13, 1993 7:00 pm*

*50 YEARS AGO*

*Led by the Rev. Wilson Woodcock, a group of 91 ministers and laymen from Greensboro area churches met with Basic Training Center No. 10 chaplains at the armed forces installation to discuss cooperation in meeting religious needs of servicemen and their families stationed in Greensboro.... Senior High School (now Grimsley) principal A.P. Routh said the school had been designated as a center for testing applicants for training as officers in the Navy V-12 Program at Chapel Hill....*

The church budget adopted in 1928 was $3,300, excluding the pastor's salary and marking $800 for missions. On May 2, 1928, the church granted a license to preach to Jeptha C. Williams, a student in the Baptist Bible Institute. This granting of a license was only the second recorded license granted to a member of the church to preach the gospel in nearly one hundred years.

# The Present Sanctuary Rises

Building started on the new auditorium with the erection of the building being completed during the ministry of Dr. N. M. Stigler. Committee members responsible for doing the planning in the area of building and finances were: R. M. Chambliss, Roy S. Moore, L. M. Short, Hugh Glass, B. Centi, G. A. Kenney, J. G. Pittman, S. J. Turner, W. H. Coffey, N. B. Keathley, W. H. Morris, William Thomas, and Jack Frain. Laying the cornerstone on July 9, 1929, the church anticipated opening the new building immediately. Services commemorating the laying of the cornerstone included Dr. M. F. Ham of Oklahoma City giving a great address on the need for preaching the gospel in your hometown.

To build the church, the church asked members to double their contributions to reach the proposed $35,000 cost of the new building. The firm of Sanders and Thomas, Inc. of Memphis was engaged to construct the building.

On July 9th 1929, the cornerstone was laid with an enclosed copper box that contained:
- Names of the officers of the church
- Names of the Officers of the Sunday School
- Names of the Deacons of the church
- A written history of the Church by S. F. Thomas and S. J. Turner
- A list of the names of the building and finance committees
- A copy of the minutes of the Big Hatchie Association on its 100th Anniversary

A picture of the pastor, Rev. N. M. Stigler and several deceased church members who were prominent in our church annals were included in the copper box in the cornerstone.

# The Stain Glass Windows Saga

Brownsville Baptist's new auditorium was so much larger and spacious than the old 1870's auditorium that the beautiful stained glass windows from the pre-1870's era would not fit the new higher and more spacious windows. However, the large window that had graced the front of the old building was the exact dimension of the newer windows. When the old church was demolished, this beautiful stained glass window, which had been given in memory of the Bond family, was disassembled piece by piece and storage was arranged in the barn of member L. M. Short. As time progressed with delay after delay in the construction of the new building and as some deaths occurred, memories were short and the location of the window's many pieces became a mystery. One of the family members, Miss Sallie Bond, who was concerned about losing her family's donation to the church, approached the widow of L.M. Short, and together they dug through the old collapsing barn and found the missing window pieces. Unfortunately, ten or more other stained glass relics from the early church windows were broken beyond repair. This occurred because when workmen tried to protect the windows, when they were stored, carefully wrapped each window and placed a layer of hay between each window. As an added cushion, they were all covered with hay to protect them from the elements. With the long delay of almost five to ten years, Mr. Short and several of the workers died. Since the windows had been stored in a barn, farm workers stored hay bales in the barn on top of the loosely-spread hay and crushed the windows. The large window was the only window that could be restored. After several months of careful reconstruction, the window was fully restored to its present form and placed on the east side of the auditorium to capture the early Sunday morning sun. A careful examination of the top of the window will note that five pieces at the apex of the window were lost in the process and had to be re-cut by the window assembly group, and evidence indicates to the viewer today that the "lost" window at the top as being slightly lighter than the sun darkened pieces that surround them. It is thought that this piece of stained glass is the oldest stained glass window in a Christian church still standing in the city today. Years later, the west window in the new auditorium was completed in memory of Mr. J. C. Duffey, who served the church as deacon. Since this last window installed cost $1,000 when completed and installed, it is thought that both of the windows are considered to be priceless. [49] In 2009, under the leadership of Mrs.

Margaret Ann Duffey, all the windows in the building were filled with beautiful stained glass scenes from the life of Jesus. Donating these windows were the families of Watts, Stewarts, Dixons, Philpotts, Callerys and Mays.

With the large open bapistry viewable from all areas of the auditorium, Miss Winifred Bumpass, a local public school art teacher, volunteered her services to paint a scene from the River Jordan in the back of the bapistry. Using a photograph provided by

---

[49] Personal conversation with members of the Bond, Short and Duffey families

one of the members who had been to the baptismal spot where Jesus was thought to have been baptized in the Jordan, "Miss Winnie", as she was known to her art students, painted a faithful representation of the site.

Several pieces of serving ware and furniture remained from the vestibule of the old church and were refinished and placed in the vestibule of the new building by the Bond family as a memorial to their parents. Only recently were some of these "relics" found and placed so that members could view them.

The old wrought iron gates and dividers from pre-Civil War days were placed in the archways leading to the auditorium balcony were removed from the old church and reinstalled in the new facility by the Coffee family.

In the old church, pews were donated by members of the church. Many of these pews were matched, refinished, and placed in the new building by their descendants. Church family members, to honor and memorialize their parents, placed additional dedicatory items like offering plates, silver serving bowls, and decorations in the church.

On Sunday March 16$^{th}$ in 1930, the doors of the new building were opened for worship. In that service, the pastor read letters from all the living former pastors voicing their support in seeing the dream of the church come to a reality. The first hymn sung in the new church was *"O For A Thousand Tongues To Sing My Great Redeemer's Praise."* The sermon of the morning was *"What Mean Ye By These Stones?"* taken from Joshua 4: 21-22, was preached by Dr. N. M. Stigler.

Among the first services was a revival held by music evangelist Ira Prosser of Fort Worth, Texas, that resulted in 46 professions of faith and 37 joining by letter. On April 2, 1930, when the soul stirring baptismal service was held, 3 additional souls were saved and were baptized at the conclusion of the service.

The church was pictured at this time in the Southern Baptist Convention's **Baptist and Reflector**, which circulated throughout the South with the heading *"Brownsville Completes A Dream."*[50]

During the times of the Great Depression, Dr. N. M. Stigler struggled financially, but faithfully served from 1928-1933. In the depression years, the struggling church issued their pastor warrants in the amount of $660 when offerings were not sufficient to pay his salary. Bro. Stigler's trials as pastor were complicated by some sorrow he experienced as indicated in the *Baptist and Reflector* on Thursday, June 16, 1930:

> *The mother of N. M. Stigler, pastor at Brownsville, G. H. Stigler, pastor at Sand Springs, Oklahoma and H. W. Stigler pastor at Fredrick, Oklahoma died Sunday morning January 5$^{th}$ at 4:00 o'clock in the home of her son in Brownsville. Her age being 74. Her husband died 34 years ago when her children were very small. Her only daughter Mrs. T. N. Miller, lives in Medina, Tennessee. She was a great and good woman and made quite a gift to God in her three sons, who all were chosen by God for the ministry. She was buried at Tumbling Creek Cemetery near Gleason, Tennessee on Tuesday morning with I. N. Penick of Jackson officiating.*[51]

Dr. Stigler left Brownsville Baptist to briefly pastor Harmony Baptist Church in the area where Haywood county and Hardeman county join. After a short pastorate there, he left to assume a teaching position at the Louisville Seminary, and in 1948 he was pastor of a church in Blackwell, Oklahoma just before his death there.

---

[50] Baptist and Reflector, March 7, 1930. Southern Baptist Press, Nashville p. 3.
[51] Baptist and Reflector, January 16, 1930. Southern Baptist Convention Press, Nashville. p.4.

# The Harwell Connection and the Moehler

The church extended a call to Rev. A. S. Harwell, who came to Brownsville from Central Church in Hot Springs, Arkansas in 1933. Rev. Harwell had been a very successful and flourishing pastor at the growing church in Hot Springs, but came to Brownsville to be near some of his family members. However after being at the church for several months in 1933, the Rev. A. S. Harwell became gravely ill. In an attempt to obtain some relief from his pain, he journeyed back to Hot Springs, Arkansas, for treatment of his illness. On July 3, 1934, the church was suddenly shocked to learn that Bro. Harwell had died in his sleep. It was during Bro. Harwell's ministry that local music teacher and church member Mrs. Lee Bond Taylor began a move to obtain funds to purchase a Moeller Organ for the church. The cost of the organ was in the neighborhood of what the original building would cost. Mrs. Taylor canvassed the community, businesses, friends and church budget to obtain the nearly $30,000 need for the purchase and installation. At the same time several other churches in the community (including First Methodist) purchased organs from the same company which lessened the price of shipping and installing the instruments. Some confusion resulted in the solicitation of funds from community residents and businesses by Mrs. Taylor, who was adamant that the organ would grace the auditorium of the church. Her perseverance paid off and the instrument of one of a kind in a church the size of Brownsville Baptist. There have been numerous organists who have graced the bench of this fine old musical instrument with the notables being Mrs. Lee Taylor, Mrs. Melissa McKenzie, Mrs. Dan Bomer, Mrs. W. H. Walker, Mr. Jeff Binford, Bro. Mike Hickman, and Mrs. Diane Mays. There were others, but these were mentioned and commended highly in the minutes of the church.

LELAND SANFORD SEDBERRY

In 2014 costs, the Moeller Organ estimated to cost about one half million dollars to be replaced. In 2010, the church refurbished the Moeller, added various new tones and qualities as all wires were replaced with electronic relays.

Rev. L. S. Sedberry came to the pulpit from Petersburg, Tennessee church near Nashville and remained pastor for three years. He was known as an eloquent speaker and became known to a church member who heard him deliver the baccalaureate sermon at Vanderbilt University in 1933 and referred him to the pulpit committee. After hearing his delivery at his church, the church voted to call him. Unexpectedly, he resigned in early 1937 to return to a Nashville church.

Bro. R. W. Roth was called upon to supply the church when Bro. Sedberry left. Bro. Roth was a radio personality in Memphis working at WMC Radio Station and known to his listeners as "Doctor Sunshine." It was during this well liked pastor's service in 1937, an interdenominational class of over 135 men organized into the Men's Bible Class, which still meets today in the church.

From a newspaper article in the Brownsville States-Graphic, dated June 25 in 1937, we read:

F. W. Roth

*"Rev. Fred W. Roth, native of New York State and has been program director of the Memphis station. For the for the past six years associated with the radio station WMC in Memphis, has accepted a call to the pastorate of the Brownsville Baptist Church. He will assume his new duties in the church in July. Known to hundreds of radio listeners in the tri-states as Doc Sunshine, for the past 18 months*

*he past three months Rev. Roth has been supply pastor of the local church. The church has been without a regular minister since the resignation of Rev. Leland Sedberry who accepted a call to the First Church in Murfreesboro, Tennessee. Rev. Roth has a wife and three sons of grammar school age. He with his family are enjoying a vacation in Waukesha, Wisconsin before assuming his active duties here. While supplying in Brownsville, Rev. Roth has made many friends. He is an able preacher and an earnest and conscientious laborer in the Master's Vineyard. The local congregation is fortunate in securing a man of his type to labor with them. He and his family will receive a welcome from the Brownsville people." (Fred W. Roth Accepts Call to Baptist Church, 1937)*

Brownsville Baptist obtained considerable notoriety during the Roth and Harwell ministries by the stand the church took in fighting the local liquor problem. A cartoon in the *Nashville Banner* on January 7, 1930 portrayed the church as a trap closed on the head of a rat. The rat was labeled "liquor sellers" and the trap bore the name of Brownsville Baptist Church snapped shut. The cartoon was labeled "A Rat's Chance!" [52]

Many members of the church credit the Pastor, R. W. Roth, along with Miss Sallie Bond as being the persons who prevented the church from falling into bankruptcy during the depression era. Miss Bond, who lost much of her farm on the church note, was instrumental in backing the trustee's loans that guaranteed the present auditorium.[53]

Stephens became pastor during the last few years of the Great dance was steady and Sunday School averaged 179, and 19 for the ples Union. Bro. Stephens had spent several years in Northern church workers from the ranks of the unemployed in order to help eir failing budgets. His efforts were plotted in Victor Irving's book, *h in the South.*[54]

Stephens tenure at the church, Earl D. Vaughn and V. A. Rose served ains in the U. S. Army and Civilian Conservation Corps.

L. A. Stephens

Evaluation of the church properties was $82,000. On February 28, 1943, atypical of the pastors who preceded him, Bro. Stephens submitted his resignation to move to a larger church to continue serving the Lord.

---

[52] The Nashville Banner. January 7, 1930. Nashville Banner Publishing, Nashville. p. 8.
[53] Notes from Emma Bond Nunn and Melissa Taylor Mackenzie 2002.
[54] Irving, Victor. *The Country Church in the South"* University of Virginia Press, 1934 p. 128.

# Changing the Worship Experience - Robert L. Orr

Dr. R.L. Orr

Coming to Brownsville Baptist from Laurel Baptist Church, Laurel, Mississippi, Dr. Robert Orr led the church from 1943-1950. Bro. Orr's pastorate was marked by increases in missions' expenditures, baptisms, church membership, and evaluation of the church property. On December 10, 1944, the church had a note-burning service to signify that all debts of the church had been paid and that the new auditorium building was finally completed and in full service. Dr. N. M. Stigler, former pastor, preached the dedicatory sermon *"People Who Dream,"* which was the sermon he preached when the building program began for the church. The 1946 budget of the church was set at an all-time high figure of $15,600.

Bro. Orr, when he arrived at Brownsville Baptist, decided to challenge some of the traditional leadership of the church. He asked the church to replace the music director because her music program was not the direction he wished to move the church evangelically. This was not an easy assignment and several confrontations with some of the family's members made the leadership of the congregation very difficult. However under Bro. Orr's direction, the church noted that attendance increased sharply with the reassigning of leadership roles in the church by the church committees. He commented, "Although some feathers were ruffled, no necks were wrung and the Lord clearly spoke to the congregation that the moves were necessary for the church to reach the community."[55]

On April 10, 1946, the church voted to take the Women's Missionary Union into the church as an official church organization with the church's full financial support. Soon thereafter, the church began on January 7, 1948, a program designed to identify and establish guidelines for the various committees of the church. This set of guidelines established the responsibilities of each committee and the primary areas of control.

As a result of his leadership of promoting the Union University while pastor at Brownsville, Dr. Orr received an honorary degree from Union University. Dr. Orr's resignation in January, 1950 ended seven years of growth and progress in the church with 300 new members added to the church rolls.

One humorous note Bro. Orr added dealt with his friendship with Bro. Jonas Stewart, who had many ties to Brownsville Baptist. It seems that Bro. Jonas being the practical joker that he was knew of Bro. Orr's affinity to southern fried chicken. His love always took the form of eating all the drumsticks he could muster when the two men were at family dinners or church dinner on the ground sessions. Once in Dallas for the Southern Baptist Convention's Pastor's Conference, Bro. Orr was a keynote speaker. It seemed that at a pre-conference luncheon that served chicken, Bro. Jonas neatly wrapped a drumstick in a napkin and without Bro. Orr's knowledge slipped the package into Bro. Orr's dress jacket's pocket. In this pocket also folded was Bro. Orr's opening sermon for the convention of hundreds of delegates. Bro. Orr related that his face was rather red as he stood before 5,000 church delegates and reached into his pocket to get his notes and found a neatly wrapped drumstick and some rather greasy notes. During Bro. Orr's

---

[55] Personal notes from conversation Robert L. Orr, 2003.

pastorate, Bro. Jonas was a frequent revivalist and was very instrumental in many Brownsvillians coming to know Jesus as Lord of their lives.[56]

After resignation, Dr. Orr pastored the First Baptist Church in Dyersburg, where he worked for twenty-five years and was instrumental in overseeing the construction of a large educational complex. His wife, Sally, was a special treat to all the ladies organizations in the church. Dr. Orr died in 2005 in Dyersburg. Much of the information about Dr. Orr comes from notes taken during a visit to Brownsville Baptist's 175th reunion.

## Short Sessions - Kelley and Harding

James Kelly

The shortest tenure as pastor of the church came with the arrival of Rev. James A. Kelly (1951) from Beverly Hills Baptist Church in Dallas, Texas, to serve in the months of July and August, 1950. By his own admission, Bro. Kelly was unhappy in Brownsville and due to the call from his home church to return, the Rev. Kelly resigned and returned to Beverly Hills Baptist Church in Fort Worth, Texas on August 20, 1950. In a conversation with an elderly lady church member, Bro. Kelly was suffering some personal health problems which necessitated his leaving Beverly Hills church. His leaving the church created a vacuum that enabled outsiders to wrestle the control of the congregation away from the Southern Baptist Convention. In defiance, the congregation sent a delegation to retrieve him "for the sake of the church.' However, he was pastor there for only a short while with the church voting to oust him and to leave the Southern Baptist Convention. Bro. Kelly then returned to the secular world to teach in public education. His death occurred just four short years later.[57]

Shortly after Bro. Kelly's departure and on October 4, 1950, the church opened its library for the first time with Betty Ruth Wilson serving as the first librarian at Brownsville Baptist Church. The church library grew in size and content and has accumulated one of the outstanding collections in this area and remains in action in late 2014 with Mrs. David Garland as exceptional librarian. The church library prides itself in its varied videotape collection on biblical sources.

After a duration of several months being served by supply pastors, Rev. Paul J. Harding (1951-1952) accepted the call to the church in late 1950. In the short few months here, several major developments occurred that affected the church life for years to come. The church called Mrs. Emma Fuson of Clifton Baptist Church in Louisville, Kentucky, to be the first educational director and full time secretary of the church on January 10, 1951. Under "Miss Emma's" tutelage, the church record-keeping entered a new phase of accountability, which has assisted later church secretaries in maintaining and storing church records. Her wisdom and clerical abilities provided each church member with an envelope system for donations and record keeping. Miss Emma was known to canvas the Sunday School classes to determine the amount of books needed by departments for the coming quarter. She was matriculate in her bulletin and newsletter preparation.

---

[56] Ibid, personal notes Orr.
[57] Personal conversation with secretary of Beverly Hills Baptist Church in Dallas, TX, May 2008.

The church budget for 1952 totaled $27,500, which set another all-time high. The old church parsonage was sold, a new one built and paid for, and plans were drawn up for the building of a new educational wing adjoining the present Sunday school building. But this growth and improvement cycle in the church was not without its costs. After this long period of strenuous activity of church growth and expansion,

Bro. Harding asked for a leave of absence for two months from church duties as pastor. The long hours of pastoring, handling the overcrowding, leading the flock and preaching left Bro. Harding with some physical difficulties, which eventually prevented his return.

## The Youthful Movement

James F. Yates

When the church received notice from Bro. Harding that he would not be returning, *(see appendix for the note)* the church called upon several members of the faculty of Union University to supply. One of the most notable supply pastors was Dr. T. O. Hall, a grandson of a former pastor. His down to earth, yet scholarly presentations of scriptures kept church members anticipating his series of continuation sermons on passages from the scripture. His May through June series on the beatitudes ended in a college printed text for student and public reading. As the church began to search diligently to find a pastor with determination to continue in the pulpit, the search committee was approached by Bro. Hall suggesting the church interview an older and rather dynamic student James Foster Yates to serve as a supply pastor on August 26, 1952. Surprisingly, Bro. Jim, as he became known to members, stirred the church by emphasizing the youth programs of the church. This philosophy paid off among the "baby boomers." Almost immediately the church posted the highest average attendance for a year, with an attendance of 430 per Sunday. Being a bachelor, Bro. Jim spent many hours working with youth and the programs of the local schools. All the youth responded and the church took on a remarkable youthful thrust in membership. The congregation was rather enthusiastic in requesting the search committee call Bro. Jim Yates as pastor. The objections to his age, his not being married and his lack of a seminary degree all were discredited and by an overwhelming vote, he was called.

The Baptist Training Union took on a decidedly youthful flavor, and enrollment reached 236 with an average attendance of 166. As children reached out to their parents and friends, the Sunday School high goal in attendance of 613 members was reached on Easter Sunday, March 29, 1953. Emphasizing this youthful look, some significant events occurred during Bro. Yates's pastorate to strengthen the life of the church. Young people in the church responded to calls of the ministry and were licensed.

On May 3, 1953, Ray Dixon was licensed to preach, and on December 8, 1955, Jimmy Douglass became the fourth minister in the history of the church to be licensed to preach.

Numerous young people made professions of faith and made their lives available for full-time Christian service. Youth night at Christmas was begun, and the yearly highlight of "Youth Week" became a standard practice for the youth to assume positions in the church from Sunday School teacher up to Youth Pastor.

Reaching outside the community, on February 9, 1955, the morning services each second Sunday morning were broadcast over WTRB in Ripley, Tennessee, and continued until June, 1956. By the middle of the 1950's, the church intensified its effort to reach out to the un-churched families in the city and county.

A city-wide census was taken by the young people to discover where the most un-churched people in the community were located. Finding that many citizens on the south side of the town were not willing to cross the railroad tracks to reach the "big church," the decision was made to start a mission.

Beginning with a Sunday school program in 1953, a group of members of the church began services in an attic room over the local Jitney Jingle Supermarket on the corner of South Washington and Margin Streets. The resultant mission became Calvary Baptist Church in late 1953 calling Harold Stanfill as pastor. Several church members went "to the mission field" and helped the church grow. Mrs. Jeanette Dixon taught the adult SS ladies class and played piano for the services. Clifford Patterson, Douglas and Martha Ann Williams were instrumental in construction projects and starting Sunday school.

During the month of November, 1955, Brownsville Baptist set a new record average attendance of 451 at the church, with an additional 51 average attendance at Calvary Baptist Chapel. The Sunday evening Training Union recorded a record 147 in attendance. Approximately two years later, on November 13, 1955, the church authorized the formation of the Calvary Baptist Chapel mission into Calvary Baptist Church. It was not long until the small congregation moved onto South Hatchie Street to build a beautiful church with Harold Stanfill as pastor. Another milestone during this time was Bro. Yates's and Joy Wirotzious marriage, which was the first marriage of a pastor during his tenure at the church. Joy joined in the activity of the church by becoming director of G.A.'s.

Again, emphasizing the continuing growth of the program, the church budget for 1956 was set at $40,000. During his tenure, Bro. Yates was working to achieve his seminary degree at Southern Baptist Seminary in Louisville, Kentucky. To do this, he boarded a train each Monday night and made his trek to the Louisville, Kentucky Southern Seminary in 1956. Bro. Yates received his seminary degree after a year of hard work and commuting to the campus. According to Bro. Yates, the 10 hour trip was not all that bad, because he and two other students studied their Greek and Hebrew enroute.

Members of the church began in 1956 to realize that additional staff people would be needed to assist the pastor in the local ministry. In early 1957 after seminary graduation, Bro. Yates resigned to accept the pastorate of First Baptist Church in Paragould, Arkansas. From Paragould, Bro. Yates moved to Yazoo City, Mississippi and pastored there until his retirement in 1991. He returned to Brownsville Baptist to preach two revivals and speak during the church's 175th anniversary. Many locals felt the sorrow and pain to discover Bro. Yates death in 2012 in Yazoo City.

While in Yazoo City, Bro. Yates set a trail of accomplishments and posts in the Mississippi as well as the Southern Baptist fields. Mr. & Mrs. Max Twiner paid Bro. Jim the ultimate praise by saying *"What a wonderful man heaven has gained. Such a gentile and loving man. You will definitely be missed."*

# Dr. Blake Westmoreland-Scholar Minister

Dr. Blake Westmoreland became pastor and served for the years of 1957 and 1958. Dr. Westmoreland's ministry was characterized for his scholarly sermons and dedication to detail in church services and finance. He resigned in late 1958 and returned to Walnut Ridge, Arkansas to teach at Williams College there. During his pastorate, the church employed Mrs. Elaine Miller to direct the music on a part-time basis. Elaine served faithfully until the church called Ray Simpson in 1960. Bro. Westmoreland left Williams College and returned to the ministry at First Baptist Church in Kerrville, Texas until his resignation and retirement in the late 1970's. Bro. Westmoreland was known for his provoking intellectual pursuits of biblical passages and conclusions drawn from "casting today alongside yesterday" in the scriptures. He was a favorite of many members of the church.

Dr. Blake Westmoreland

His series on "Latter Day Saints" became a favorite where and whenever he preached the seven part series.

# H.K. Sorrell - A Lengthy Pastorate

The progression of growth begun in the 1950's continued under the leadership of Dr. H. K. Sorrell, who came in 1959 from Kentucky. Church attendance in 1959-60 was 515 in Sunday school and 104 in Training Union.

Although the church had had a men's organization since the early 1860's, the church began a formal brotherhood with a dinner on June 15, 1959, with 30 joining the organization. The first director of the Brotherhood was Harrell Clement. The membership of the Brotherhood soon reached 72 men, and Harrell Clement became the director of the Big Hatchie Baptist Brotherhood Association, the following year.

*H. K. Sorrell*

The Lottie Moon Christmas offering reached $1,557.53 in the 1959 Christmas season. Under the leadership of Dr. H. K. Sorrell, the church was instrumental in the development of Poplar Corner Baptist Church in 1969.

Land west of the city of Brownsville near the site of the original Russell Springs Church was purchased for future expansion to the west of the city. Continued physical growth of the church plant continued an in February, 1960, the church acquired the Thornton property north of the church for $6,500. During March, 1960, the church sought to form a new Baptist Association composed of Haywood and Crockett County churches.

Bro. Sorrell received an honorary doctorate from Union University for his services to the university. He became a world traveler with members of the church as tours took them across the United States, Europe and Israel. Hundreds of his parishioners thoroughly enjoyed the informative and breath taking views possible by such tours, cruises and pilgrimages. One of these ventures took twenty-five church members and guests to the Baptist World Alliance in Stockholm, Sweden in 1974.

During March, the church voted to call Mr. Ray Simpson to join the staff as the first full-time minister of music. Mr. Ray Simpson served the church well from 1960 to 1963. Ministers of Music that followed Ray Simpson were:

| | |
|---|---|
| Phillip Sherrod | 1963-1969 |
| Larry Flanagan | 1970-1973 |
| Doug Jernigan | 1973-1973 |
| Kenny Bryan | 1974-1975 |
| Bob Matthews | 1975-1980 |
| Jack Horner | 1981- 1982 |
| Ralph Brown | 1982- 2000 |
| Ken Hall | 2001- 2008 |
| Walter Brinks | 2010 - |

In 1973, an additional full-time staff member was called to serve as the Minister of Education. Paul E. Young assumed that position for 1973-1975.

In April, 1960, the church maintained an all-time high average of 556 members in Sunday School, with 81 visitors. The Brotherhood reached a total of 81 members that held cottage-style prayer meetings for church members. In the following month of June, the church appointed a committee to investigate the beginning of a kindergarten for Brownsville Baptist Church members. By December, 1960, church average attendance moved upward to 538 in Sunday School with 301 visitors during the services.
The church budget for the 1962 was $65,000.

In November, 1961, Mrs. Sue Short, who had served since Miss Emma Fuson's retirement, resigned as church secretary. Mrs. Mary Ann Stewart was selected as the third full-time church secretary.

The Brotherhood began a monthly visit to the wards at Western State Mental Hospital in November, 1961.

In April, 1962, another attendance record was broken in average Sunday School attendance with 586 members present. There were 723 members present on Easter Sunday, 1962. Again more records were broken in June, 1962, with attendance in May averaging 609 present per Sunday in Sunday School, and an average of 132 in Training Union.

In July, 1962, the church broke ground on a 12,000 square foot addition to accommodate 800 Sunday School members at a cost of $150,000. In September, 1962, the church purchased the lots facing West College Street from Mrs. Homer Rainey for a price of $15,000, which led the church to propose a budget for 1963 of $70,000. Continued increases in the Sunday School report topped again in May, 1963, with an average attendance of 619 in Sunday School, which was matched by a total of 149 all-time high in Training Union.

On May 22, 1963, Bro. Ray Simpson resigned to join Oakhurst Baptist Church in Clarksdale, Mississippi, as minister of Music and Education. On July 31, 1963, the church called Bro. Philip Sherrod from Hunt, Texas, as the new Minister of Music.

The budget for 1964 was $75,000, with the average attendance in Sunday School reaching a 638, which remained until January, 1965, when the attendance dropped to a 604 average. The Training Union figures were much better showing an average of 154.

On May 5, 1965, the church began two worship services on Sunday mornings with one beginning at 8:30 and the other at 11:00.

The church purchased two lots on Boyd Avenue to begin exploration of a mission in east Brownsville on July 14, 1965. On October 1, 1965, the church elected Mrs. Clayton Richardson to be the new church secretary.

Following Mrs. Richardson's retirement, Mrs. Carolyn Rains Nelson served faithfully for many years and the present secretary called in 2014 is Mrs. Cheryl Halliburton. The church proposed a $100,000 budget for the 1965-66 year.

In 2017, the church called Mrs. Debbie Barnes to be the secretary, who proved to be most efficient in assuming the authorship of the church newsletter and maintaining the church's website on the internet.

# Spreading Out The Baptist Influence

The church began on April 1, 1966, to broadcast the Sunday evening services of the church over the local radio station. Poplar Corner Baptist Mission grew into a reality and began a Sunday School and Worship Service schedule in April, 1966. Bro. Max Cannon was called to be the first pastor of the mission.

A study committee was appointed in September, 1966, to start the formation of the Haywood Baptist Association.

In 1968, a major controversy erupted in the church family with the pastor of the Poplar Corner Mission joining a new Baptist movement in north Mississippi, which the deacons and fellowship of the church felt would be detrimental to the support of foreign missions in Brownsville Baptist Church. Since the church had been founded on support to missions, the pastor of the mission was asked to resign. Thirty members and the pastor founded Fellowship Baptist Church and their names were removed from the church rolls. Poplar Corner Church has continued to grow since this controversy to be the second largest church in the city in 1990. Bro. Lamar Boothe became the pastor of the mission in February, 1968.

In July, 1969, the church voted to allow the private school, Tennessee Academy, to use the facilities of the church for one year in order to organize and begin a private school for students of Haywood County.

In 1981, the church purchased from the estate of E. E. Walker, a brick house on the corner of West College and Wilson, for our returning missionary families. The dwelling was renovated throughout and has been a source of delight to the congregation and missionary families. In that same year, the church began a Child Development Center on the corner of Franklin and Russell Streets. Soon after this purchase, the church purchased the house next door which was known as the Worthy House.

In 1988, Dr. H. K. Sorrell retired after 30 years of service as pastor of Brownsville Baptist Church. Dr. Sorrell fills the distinction as the longest serving pastor of this 175-year-old congregation. Major contributions to the church during Dr. Sorrell's 30 years of service include:

- *Home purchased on Park Avenue for Minister of Music/Education*
- *Multipurpose section of Educational Building is constructed*
- *A Kindergarten program in the fall of 1963*
- *Two Sunday morning worship services started in 1965*
- *Haywood Baptist Association is organized in 1967*
- *Poplar Corner Mission becomes a church in 1969*
- *Barry Presley licensed to preach in 1970*
- *Rotation of Deacons Program begun on March 10, 1971*
- *Paul Young is hired as the first full-time Minister of Education hired in 1972*
- *Paul Young licensed to preach on December 6, 1972*
- *Property expansion and building program to raise church property evaluation of over $1,000,000*
- *Church-wide visitation program on a weekly basis*
- *Hospital and nursing home visitation program*
- *Live Longer and Like It Organization for older adults organized*

- *Puppet Ministry is organized in 1974*
- *Stephen Williams ordained to preach on May 30, 1976*
- *Union University bestows a Doctor of Divinity degree on H.K. Sorrell in 1975*
- *Dr. Sorrell and church group attend Baptist World Alliance in Stockholm, Sweden in 1975*
- *First Adult Retreat held in Eureka Springs, Arkansas, in 1979.*
- *Child Development Center opens and a Missionary Home is purchased in 1981.*
- *Union University Scholarship Program for church youth is organized in 1983.*
- *Church multipurpose room undergoes extensive remodeling in 1983*
- *Church expands its missions by hiring Dr. Manuel Valdez as part time minister to work with Hispanics in county in 1983.*
- *Church continues expansion in ministry by starting a deaf ministry in 1983.*
- *Church votes to build Family Life Center in 1984*
- *Church begins pre-school program in 1985.*
- *Production Credit Administration building is purchased by the church in 1987, pastorium is deeded to pastor, and Brownsville Baptist Shelter for homeless itinerants established in 1987*
- *Haywood Baptist Association building is completed in 1988.*
- *Church budget reached the $462,000 mark in October 1988.*
- *During Dr. Sorrell's term as pastor, Ray Dixon, Jim Douglass, Dorothy Frady, Doug McDurham, Dan Spencer, Frank Fawcett, Van Spencer, Barry Presley, Bill Sorrell, Stephen Sorrell, Robert Waggener, Stephen Sorrell all volunteered for some phase of religious services.[iv]*

Realizing that the building and church facilities were not capable of housing the ever-growing population, the church voted on Sunday, February 19, 1989, after the morning worship service to begin construction on a Family Life Center for the church at a cost of $802,840. According to Dr. Sorrell, this had been one of the dreams of the church for some time, and with generous donations from several church members in addition to extra tithing by the congregation, the building program began.

Shortly after Dr. Sorrell's retirement, David Hicks was licensed to preach in 1989. As the church searched for a pastor, Dr. Robert Elliott of Union University served as Interim Pastor and drew large crowds and provided a wonderful atmosphere for continued growth and development in the church.

# The Current Connerley Era

With the search committee seeking pastors from across the convention, they turned to Rev. Bob Connerley from Grenada, Mississippi who became pastor in 1989. Bro. Connerley was a graduate of Southwestern Baptist Theological Seminary in Fort Worth, Texas and had been pastoring in his home state of Mississippi until called by Brownsville Baptist.

Shortly after arrival, the mew pastor led the church to call Mike Hickman as the first Minister of Activities. Mike was asked to spearhead the planning for the new Family Life Center, which was completed and occupied on January 18, 1990. Assisting Mike Hickman in this undertaking was the planning committee of Clyde Stewart, Mrs. Fred Gause, John Gorman, Jr., Carl Gruenewald, Bill Presley, Mrs. Ronnie Richards, Mr. R. E. Scott, Mrs. Pauline Spencer, and Steve Wimberly. Due to additions and equipment, the Family Life Center was completed in January, 1990, at a cost of $888,308.00. The building committee for the construction consisted of Jerry Stoots, Carl Gruenewald, Bill Gruenewald, John Gorman, Sr., Dr. H. K. Sorrell, Jerry Hartfield (Architect), and Ralph Chandler (Contractor). With the decisive determination of the congregation, the 20 year note was paid off on the Family Life Center in just seven years.

On March 7, 1990, the church authorized the development of a Spanish Mission Ministry at the church with a budget of $5,046.70 in partnership with the Tennessee Baptist Convention and the Haywood Baptist Association. Spearheading the effort in the church was Mrs. Mary Williams, who was a retired minister's wife. Through her hard work and diligence, the church was able to start a Hispanic Sunday School for migrant workers who were arriving in Haywood County and Brownsville to work in the farming community. The Spanish group met in the PCA building, which the church purchased to be used in their Sunday School.

On May 21, 1990, the church revised its policies and articles to incorporate changes in the articles of faith, election of deacons, standing committee's responsibilities, and schedules for employees and meetings. This reorganization was the first complete revision in the history of the church, which was necessary due to the growth and size of the church organization. It was decided by the church to establish a limited licensed corporation to protect the entity from lawsuits.

In April, 1991, the church authorized support for its first Women's Conference at the church by approving $500 for expenses in a May 4th conference. In March, 1991, the church purchased additional parking space behind Spencer's Clinic. The church purchased new hymnals for the auditorium by members purchasing individual hymnals as memorials or to honor loved ones.

Beginning in 1992, ten members of the church joined a missionary trip to Philippines, where they built churches and started Bible study among the Philippine people.

Locally, the men of the church assisted and organized a new Boy Scout troop in February, 1992. With the resignation of Mike Hickman as Activities Director in April, 1992, the church voted to accept $30,000 for the Lebanon Road properties from Fellowship Baptist Church and to apply the amount on the outstanding note on the Family Life Center.

The church was fortunate in July, 1992, to have Paul Bowman to accept the call to serve as Minister of Activities and Education. In September, 1993, the church purchased a new 29-passenger mini-bus and a 15-passenger van for use in the church transportation ministry. Paul Bowman and Ralph Brown were instrumental in securing church vehicles to replace the older worn-out bus and vans with newer models. Members of the church began a series of retreats and trips to take advantage of the new travel opportunities.

*2016 Church Staff*

In October, 1992, the church voted to give $3,000 to Rev. Joe and Gloria Turman to assist in building a church in Livingstone, Zambia, where the two missionaries serve. The church was completed just prior to the Turmans being forced to leave Zambia due to religious struggles between the Muslims and Christians in the country.

Bill Gruenewald was ordained to the gospel ministry on April 18, 1993. On June 20, 1993, the church voted to renovate the church auditorium at a cost of $57,980. Total church receipts reached $651,000 for the year of 1993-1994. The proposed budget for the 1994-1995 church year reached $667,000, and church property value reached the $2,000,000 mark.

In June, 1995, the church voted to support and send B. J. Sanford to China on a sports/mission trip and Elizabeth Turman to Indonesia for a language training school on summer missions programs.

. Over the five-year period from 1985 to 1990, church members participated in mission trips to Honduras and Mexico. Some of the youth joined with adults from the community to ride their bicycles to Mexico for missions. Youth groups were formed to encourage Bible reading in the public schools, and Brownsville Baptist youth were very active in these organizations

A full-time minister, Bro. Mario Maldonaldo was called in April, 1996, to minister to the Hispanic congregation that was beginning to move into the community. The Hispanic church has grown dramatically in membership to near 75 members, and moved into the renovated basement of the Sunday School building . In May, 1997, in an agreement between the Spanish ministry of the church and a local radio station, the church agreed to assume the operations of WNWS-Am radio station for the Hispanic evangelization of the West Tennessee area. . With the growth of the Hispanic church, the church employed an associate pastor, Bro. David Herrera, to assist in the Hispanic church program on July 11, 1999.

On August 30, 1998 the church employed Mrs. Carolyn Nelson as Administrative secretary, and assigned Miss Betty Jo Goff to be Financial Secretary. In addition the church employed Mrs. Jan Yates to be the outreach secretary on a part time basis.

The church purchased the Waymon Worthy home on West College Street for $52,500.

The church voted on September 27, 1998, to incorporate itself as Brownsville Baptist Church and register with the state as an incorporated religious association.

For the first time in history, the receipts for the 1999 year surpassed the million dollar mark at $1,015,976.

Because of the resignation of Paul Bowman, the church decided to open a new position on the staff, Minister to Families. Because of the unique character of this position, the church desired a minister, who related to all groups within the congregation. Realizing that the church already possessed such a minister, Bro. Ralph Brown retired as

Minister of Music and was appointed Minister to Families. With Bro. Brown's resignation in 2006, the church called Bro. Jason Smith who served until 2011.

Bro. George Norvell was appointed to serve as Interim Minister of Music during the search committee's efforts to secure a new Minister of Music. Serving on the committee for securing the minister of music were: Danny Presley, Steve May, Polly Stewart, Ray Dixon, and Vickie Garrett. The committee selected Walter Brinks from Hueytown, Alabama who began in 2010.

On Sunday, June 18, 2000, Bro. Mario Maldonado resigned as pastor of the Hispanic Church to accept a position with the North American Mission Board to assist in evangelizing the Hispanic community in Tennessee. Bro. David Herrera, Assistant Pastor, was asked to serve as interim pastor the Hispanic Church. The Hispanic Church in 2010 purchased the building on East Main Street formerly used by the Church of Christ and had a note burning of the debt in 2011.

Members of the church in April of 2000 decided to prepare a month long celebration to commemorate the 175th Anniversary of the Brownsville Baptist Church. The committee appointed to this celebration are: Patricia Gruenewald, Chairman; Billy Garrett; Ray Dixon; Millie Richards, and Jan Mills.

The Celebration of 175th Anniversary included a return of several pastors from the past, uniting with long lost members, large numbers of visitors and stirring sermons celebrating the church activity over the years.

Continuing under the leadership of Bob Connerley, the church for several years experienced an increase in attendance in most all services. Baptisms were up, Sunday School attendance maintained a steady pace and finances were well within balance showing surpluses in most areas. Very importantly to deacons, the annual budget was being met and some reserve was being built.

Several major plant projects took place in the years 2011-2014, with the addition of a youth department in the basement area previously occupied by the Hispanic Church, who had vacated for the East Main Street property. With the resignation of Bro. Jason Smith to begin a church planting activity in the Northwest, a committee consisting of Billy Garrett, Robbie Russell, Crystal Parker, Jim Reason an Regan Baumheckel was formed to seek a Minister of Students.

The church called Bro. Mike Young to be minister to students with the resignation of Bro. Jason Smith. It was decided to drop the position of Ministers to Families to accommodate the acquisition of Bros. Smith and then Bro. Young to direct the youth program of the church. Bro. Young's first major project was the converting of the basement area in to a site to be called "The Youth Place." It consisted of a group area, classrooms, kitchen and cafe type atmosphere which the young people seemed to like and flocked to the program.

Another project was undertaken with funds from an anonymous donor to build a portico on the northeast entrance to the Family Life Center and Sunday School area. A beautiful entrance way was constructed to allow automobiles to bring church members up to the doors and out of the weather to enter the building. To accompany this "dry weather entrance" a couple of additions were made to the entrance to the main auditorium by providing a sheltered entrance on the East Side for those choosing to enter from this side of the church to the sanctuary. On the west side a covered ramp was constructed to lead from the lower floor of the Sunday School area to the sanctuary to avoid the steps which were required from the first floor level to the sanctuary. To modify these additions, a security system was installed which enabled the doors to be locked to the outside once services were begun, but open upon need to exit the building.

Another renovation that occurred was the total reconstruction of the interior of the Fellowship Hall. With the modernization of the kitchen, addition of a food service plateau, and beautiful carpet added to the floor, the area was beautifully decorated with wall covering and hangings of scripture verses. Much of the work and planning from the church plant committee fell into the willing and dedicated hands of Mrs. Margaret Ann Duffey, who carefully oversaw the efforts. Much of this work was done with funds from the church and anonymous donors.

In 2014, the church decided to revamp the entire second floor of the Sunday School building to incorporate children's church section in addition to remodeling the spaces for several classes of young adults. Using the capabilities of Carl Gruenewald, who was a plant director in Pictsweet Corporation, the project was contracted and set into motion. The theme for the floor was built around the tremendous art work of Rev. Chris Alsup, who was an artist and church planter located in Hawaii.

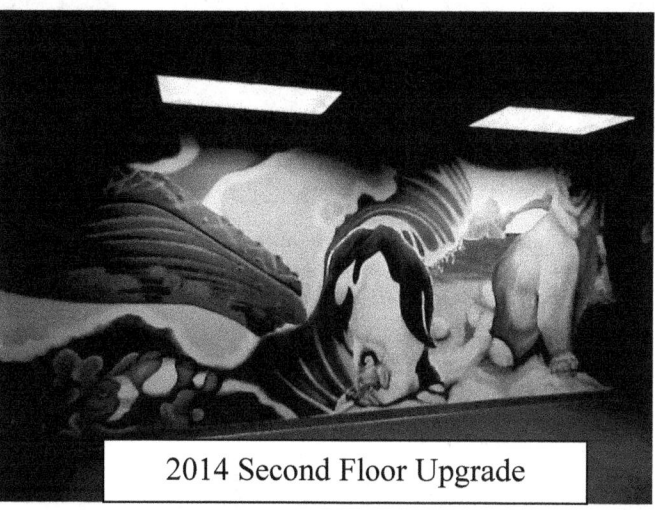

2014 Second Floor Upgrade

Rev. Alsup constructed the artwork for the project in his studio in Hawaii and shipped it to Brownsville, where he came and installed the portions of the work on the walls to give the design a favorable "Bible story" look to the four year old through the sixth grade occupants. The funding for the project was received from several of the trusts income to the church to develop the buildings and church plant. A state of the art teaching facility was created for this children's age group.

Starting in 2014 also, the church established a website with Ray Dixon as webmaster. Each year since 1990, the sanctuary choir has presented a gift to the community in the acclaimed **"Carols of Christmas."** Hundreds have joined for two to four night performances of the choir as they recreate the music of Christmas. Highlighting these performances on occasion, George Norvell and the drama department of the church provide realistic visions of the Christian experience.

Brownsville Baptist Church has reaped the benefits of having able and efficient men of God who blessed the church with their dedication and service over the 175 years of church history. It is very unusual for a church of this age to have a complete list of those who have stood in the pulpit and preached the Gospel with power for these 175 years. The success of this church is due largely to the efforts of these men of God who faithfully preached the gospel to a willing congregation.

This history could not be closed without expressed appreciation for Bro. Bob Connerley, who is the pastor of Brownsville Baptist Church for the past 28 years. Bro. Connerley has been an adept preacher, theologian and administrator who has seen the continual rise in church efforts in the community. He and Bro. Sorrell compose a fifty year history of the church and deserve appreciation by the community for their tireless efforts to elevate the standards of the church and congregation.

---

[1] Autobiography found in "The History of Lauderdale County, Tennessee, The Goodspeed Publishing Company 1886.

*Role Playing Gives Bible Students A Vision of Biblical Times*

*Choir in 2018 Sings Anthem of Praise*

*Stained Glass Window found in Balcony Window*

*Vivid Scene from many theatrical productions at BBC*

*Youth Project in 2016*

*Late 1940's Vacation Bible School*

# Appendix: Documents from Brownsville Baptist Church Files

THE INTERIOR JOURNAL, STANFORD, LINCOLN COUNTY, KENTUCKY, FRIDAY, DECEMBER 23, 1910 Digital Library, Kentuckiana Digital Library.

---

[iii] *Personal Correspondence from Walter Knox Limyard to the author.*

---

[iv] ***Excerpts from Biographies of Tennessee Baptist Ministers***

---

***Argument Presented by Peter Smith Gayle to His Big Hatchie Circular Letter:***

Authors note: Landmarkism (Baptist only will be saved) pervaded the faith in the early years of Brownsville Baptist. It was a general mode across the frontier and settlement areas in Western Tennessee, and to word or change anything that might be different was often charged as "modernism." It is in this argument that Pastor Peter Gayle presented this thesis:

"I could not have believed, without proof, that any one, at least in this age and country, could have doubted the positions here assumed, First, that Jehovah intends to save sinners. Second, that he works by means. Third, that all the knowledge of man is received through the senses. Fourth, that all the means used by God, are exerted on man through the senses.

If those persons who rejected this letter, understood themselves, they evidently deny by their conduct all the above named positions except the first. Reader, if these three last positions be false, the proof must rest either on their infallibility, or the Scriptures. They did not decide on ground of infallibility; for they made no such lofty pretensions And, since the Scriptures are couched in language addressed to the understanding, can you imagine how one can comprehend them, unless through the senses? Therefore, the following conclusion is inevitable: they must have called into exercise their senses; and thus annihilate their own vote and establish my positions.

It may be urged as a dernier resort, by those who cannot meet arguments that the doctrines taught in this circular is Campbellism; and just so doing excite the prejudice of both believers and unbelievers against me. This is an easy way, but most unfair way, of escaping the force of truth and it is becoming quite customary in these days of slander and reproach to cry out Campbellism! Campbellism!, against those who press them constantly with the force of Scripture, thus endeavoring to destroy by an opprobrious nick-name, those whom they were unable to overcome in argument.

Now, without taking upon myself to decide what Mr. Campbell does or does not teach, the doctrine of Divine agency accompanying the use of means, is too clearly set forth in the foregoing circular, to require of me any further affirmation; (while that which is called Campbellism denies the doctrine of all Divine agency, other than that contained in the means alone,) on the contrary the circular declares God's truth and God's agency to be two things, and that the former is exerted through the latter, making all means effectual, without which Divine influence, they never would produce a single conversion."

The circular letter and vindication being too lengthy to appear entire, the author has only given a portion of the vindication; sufficient as he supposes, to give the views contained in said letter.

To show the appreciation in which he was held, the writer thinks it not inappropriate to copy from a public journal the following tribute of respect, passed by the Clinton and Madison Masonic Lodges:

On yesterday, the 8th day of June, a gentle spirit passed away. It has taken its upward flight to dwell forever in the bosom of its Father and its God, there to associate with kindred excellence; there to reap the reward of a well spent life; there divested of the cross of frail mortality, its cares and sorrows, to wear the unfading garments of an undying eternity, and to live forever in realms of life and everlasting bliss.

Yes brethren a watchman has taken on the walls of Zion in the discharge of his duties, he having long stood there and proclaimed the un-searchable riches of the gospel of Christ, and as we are credibly informed, has spent a handsome fortune in the service of his Divine Master, in building of churches and paying ministers, he at the same time being a minister and entitled to receive wages; for we are told 'the laborer is worthy of his hire' Yes, he has fallen amidst one of the greatest revivals of religion we have ever had in the village of Clinton, he being the principal agent in bringing it about.

Rev. Peter S. Gayle, our brother, is no longer on earth; he has left us to join a nobler association on high. He has gone; his bodily presence has left its, but the undying influence of his character and example still are ours, still to incite us in our labors of love; still to whisper peace in our halls. May we emulate his virtues here, so that we may join him above. Therefore,

Be it Resolved, That in the death of Brother Gayle society has been deprived of one of its best and most useful members; the Baptist church of a distinguished and devoted minister, and Masonry of one who cherished the ~ principles of our Order.

- Resolved, That we tender to the family of the deceased brother our warmest and most heartfelt sympathies in their affliction.

-Resolved, That in testimony of our respect to the memory of our deceased brother, this Lodge and its members shall be clothed in mourning thirty days.

-Resolved, That a copy of this preamble and resolutions be forwarded to the family of the deceased, and that they be published in the Hinds County Gazette, at Raymond; The Tennessee Baptist, at Nashville; The Western Recorder, at Louisville, and The Mississippian and Flag of Our Union, at Jackson, Miss.

By order of the Madison Lodge, No. 73.     J. J. SCOTT, W. M.
M. G. JOHNSON, Sec'y.

As intimated above, Elder Gayle sacrificed much for the 'cause of Christ'. He came to Tennessee at the time of the great conflict between the Antinomian and Missionary parties. Being decidedly "an effort man," (as the missionary was called in those days), he wielded a powerful and widespread influence in favor of missions, at home and abroad. He was one, of the originators of the Baptist State convention, which finally resolved itself into the West Tennessee Baptist convention, of which he was a member, and of which he was~ president for a number of years—up to the time of his leaving the State.

Elder Gale was like others; he had his enemies, even in the ranks of those who professed to be his friends. His doctrines were misrepresented and distorted. He was requested by the Big Hatchie association, at its session in 1838, to prepare a circular letter for its session in 1839, with which he complied; but, when read, called forth great opposition, and was finally rejected, as being unsound. The context of this argument can be found in the appendix and indicates the depth and comprehension of the gospel held by Br. Gayle.

Elder Gayle was above the medium size, somewhat stooped in his shoulders, of pleasing address, usually wearing a smile, especially while preaching. The biographer was baptized by him, at Covington, Tenn., August 17, 1837. He will never forget the pleasant smile he wore upon the occasion. He remarked, while in the water, (a pleasant smile beaming from his countenance,) "It is always pleasant to obey Jesus Christ." His whole soul seemed to be absorbed in his Master's business.

He was the father of eight children. Thomas C., Almira E., William H., Sarah, Mary, Fannie, Jennie and Ella; two of whom are dead—William and Mary. The six living are all Baptists.

Elder Gayle was in the organization of the first Baptist education society in West Tennessee, (if not in the State) formed at Brownsville, Haywood county, July 26, 1835, of which he was made the agent. This last item of his history is found in the Baptist Triennial Register for 1836.

But few of the noble band who formed this society are now alive. Only Thomas Owen, R. S. Thomas, L. H. Bethel and James G. Hall. The others are resting from their labors, and their works are following them.

Elder Gayle was one of the originators of the first State convention, organized at Mill Creek church, Davidson county, 1833, and was the first president of the West Tennessee Baptist convention.[iv]

* Contributed by Elder W. C. Gilbert.

# Champ C. Conner

## "ANOTHER GREAT MAN IN ISRAEL FALLEN."

At a meeting of brethren representing Elim, Grace, Ripley, Society Hill and Woodlawn churches, in the town of Ripley, February 20th, 1875, Elder Joseph H. Borum was called to the chair, and Brother P. T. Glass to act as secretary. The following was passed:

"Elder Champ Carter Conner, D. D., the son of John Conner, was born in Culpepper county, Va., March 13, 1811, and was baptized by Elder Cumberland George into the fellowship of the Broad Run Baptist church, Fauquier county, Va., September 14th, 1828, and very soon thereafter commenced preaching the gospel, being in his eighteenth year. He married Ann Eliza Slaughter, December 23, 1833, and moved to West Tennessee in November, 1835; died at Indian Mound, (the place of his residence) Lauderdale county, Tenn., February 14, 1875. He was an able parliamentarian and presiding officer over deliberative bodies; nearly always, when present at the Big Hatchie association and West Tennessee Baptist convention, was chosen to fill the chair as moderator and president, presiding with dignity and precision upon all occasions. He possessed rare talent as a minister of the gospel; of almost unequaled eloquence, he could hold his audience spell bound for hours, and was an able defender [champion] truly of Baptist doctrine and practice, contending always most "earnestly for the faith once delivered to the saints." He was a "land marker," both in faith and practice, yet, while he was hold and fearless in the advocacy of the doctrines he held, he was always courteous and respectful to those who differed with him. He was not only gifted as a preacher, but was a man of acquirements, having given considerable attention to both medicine and jurisprudence, and also to matters appertaining to the affairs of State and National governments. At the time of his decease he was pastor of four churches— Grace, Society Hill, Woodlawn and Zion. So he died in the field assigned by the Master, with harness fully on—"died at his post," and has left a large vacuum in the denomination, which can not be easily filled. We shall miss him in the community as a citizen; in the neighborhood as a kind neighbor. We shall miss him at our social gatherings, we shall miss him at our churches; we shall miss him at our anniversaries; and, oh, bow he will be missed in the family and at the domestic altar!

> "But he is gone to receive his reward, having left us in his sixty-fourth year, after a few days of suffering, which he bore with becoming resignation, to join the company of the redeemed, to swell the anthem of redeeming grace and undying love."

> "Servant of God well done;
> Rest from thy toyed employ;
> The battle fought, the victory won,
> Enter thy Master's joy.
> Soldier of Christ well done;
> Praise be thy new employ;
> And while eternal ages run,
> Rest in thy Savior's joy."

*"Resolved,* That in the death of Elder Champ C. Conner the church of Christ has lost a great and good man, and the community a valued citizen.

*"Resolved,* That while we bow with submission to this bereavement of Providence, we deeply sympathize with the dear afflicted family in the irreparable loss they have sustained, hut feel assured that for our Brother Conner to die is gain, yea, great gain to him.

*"Resolved,* That a copy of these proceedings he furnished the hereaved family, The Ripley News and The Baptist, with the request that The Religious Herald, Wessern Recorder, Western Baptist, and Ford's Christian Repository copy, and that the same be spread upon the church hook of Ripley, of which he was a member at the time of his death.

JOSEPH H. BORUM, *Moderator.*
P. T. **GLASS,** *Secretary.*

There were brethren present from the several churches mentioned, which gave tone and character to the meeting.

Brother Conner possessed social qualities in a high degree; possessed a sprightly intellect; enjoyed a good joke; could join in a hearty laugh with his friends; was good at repartee; clear and forcible in an argument. He had a debate at one time with a Presiding Eider, in Gibson county, in which, I understood, he showed considerable skill as a logician and polemic. His piety increased with his years. It was very perceivable to me. The change was manifestly great.

There was more of humility, meekness, submission, patience and diligence in the Master's service than formerly.

He would frequently say that his work was most done. He died of pneumonia. I saw him but once during his illness. At the time he was not thought to be dangerous. He was a bold, uncompromising Baptist. Some thought atone time that he was tinctured with Campbellism, but that was a mistake. I often heard him say that if he were not a Baptist he would be an infidel, and would explain himself by saying the Bible was so plain in its distinctive teachings that honest men were bound to be Baptists. He was utterly opposed to pulpit affiliations with teachers of error. This sentiment grew and strengthened up to the day of his death. He was a great friend of missions and Sabbath-schools. Being one of the pioneer preachers in West Tennessee, he had to meet and combat Anti-Nomianism in all its varied forms; but he lived to see it almost extinct. Now and then, here and there, a few charred remains can be seen, at remote distances apart, exhibiting clearly that fake is written upon it, and that it will soon pass away. Brother Conner helped to bury it in this country. He was called to preside, for a term of years, as the President of the Baptist Female College, at Hernando, Miss.

I do not remember how many. He was also the pastor of the Hernando church several years. He served as the pastor of Brownsville church some time. He was called at one time as the pastor of St. Francis Street Baptist church, Mobile, but from some cause did not accept.

His talents were not so well adapted to the pastorate as they were to that of the evangelist, however. Upon the whole, he was a man and minister of brilliant parts, rarely met with.

But the orator is gone! We shall hear no more his soft, mellow voice, or see the melting eye or falling tear, (he often wept), while preaching. That tongue lies silent at Indian Mound. Those eyes weep not there amidst the pine, the cedar, and the box, as they used to do when pleading with sinners to become reconciled to God. There were some subjects, he told me, he could not in his later years preach about. One was: "The awful condemnation of the finally impenitent." While preaching from the text: "If the righteous scarcely be saved, where shall the ungodly appear ?" his mind was seized with such inconceivable horror that he had to desist and retire from the subject, his mind being filled with the fearful consequences of the damned in hell. Oh, what a fearful thought!

The following letters—the first addressed to his mother, shortly after his conversion, in his eighteenth year; the other to the author eleven months before his death, will be, doubtless, read with interest by his numerous friends and relatives:

> **NEW BALTIMORE, August** 5, 1881 Dearest Mother, I have not heard from you when I wrote upon the glorious subject of religion. But I have been disappointed ; not one line have I had from father, mother, sister or brother. All of them except my dear mother appear to be strangers to the love of their brother. You have given me good advice, which I will follow if God is willing. You have been as good and kind to me as a mother should be to a child, and indeed I think as much so as one could he, and for this reason I know have a good excuse for not writing to your absent son, which one day he will know. Perhaps you think he has just received a momentary warning of his lost and undone situation, or you may think what you may say to him may make him join the church too soon, and then afterwards he kill repent of having done it. But my mother shall never repent of having urged me to join, for one hour spent in the service of my Lord is worth years of sin, and I consider it my duty to join, therefore, I shall offer my experience next Saturday~ if my heart does not fail me. But I am afraid I shall not be received. I am afraid they will say 'go away, young man,

## Upon receiving a proposal to form a Church Association in the river plain of the Hatchie River, Bro. Champ Conner voices his concern:

> INDIAN MOUND, TENN., March 13, 1874.
> *Rev. Joseph IL Borum:*

VERY DEAR BROTHER—From some hints I have heard out in the country I fear there is a plan on foot to propose the union of all sorts of professed Christians, in Ripley, in what is falsely called 'a union meeting,' and so to arrange it that you, as a consistent man, can not take part in it, and then to use your refusal against you and against the Baptist church, which is the church of Christ. Hence, I write to put you on your guard. It does seem that the devil has gotten tired of openly dividing the Baptist church, and that now his aim is to divide it by the professed union of opposite sentiments, tinder the cloak of Christian love. A Methodist, with his salvation by works, rejoicing in his ability to fall from grace, and one day to he palpably the child of God, and the next to be the child of the devil—a Presbyterian, opposing both these, but an extremist in fatality; making God the author of sin—a Cumberland, claiming a church that is no older than ourselves and having David Ewing as its head rather than Christ, whilst John Calvin is the Presbyterian, exalted above Jesus of Nazareth, John Wesley is, by the Methodists, exalted as equal with God, and each, and all, and every one of them proposing to convert and to save the soul by a few drops of water, together they come, and in professedly deep anxiety, wish to unite with the mean, low-lived, narrow-minded, bigoted Baptists, to convert and save a community of sinners. Unite in what? Can cold soon be added to hot? Can truth and falsehood dwell in harmony? There is hypocrisy in all such propositions. For several weeks I have been going to your house on Wednesday, as Thursday most likely to catch you at home, but from various causes have been prevented from doing so. I suffer very much with neuralgia in my right shoulder, and write with difficulty. I am about starting to Zion, and must close this hasty epistle. Today I am sixty-three years old. Love to all of the family.

Affectionately yours,     CHAMP C. CONNER.

## Presentations in the Biography of Early Baptist Ministers:

### WILLIAM P. BOND.

Elder Wm. P. Bond, son of Lewis Bond, was born in Bertie county, N. C., October 16, 1813. He professed religion at Chapel Hill in 1831, and was baptized by Dr. Hooper; united with Mount Carmel church 1832; married Lucy Rascoe in 1835 moved to Tennessee in 1837. and settled in Brownsville and engaged in the legal profession; was elected judge of the circuit court in 1865, which he held up to 1871.

January 1871, was ordained to the gospel ministry;
Presbytery: Elders G W. Young, Mat. Hillsman, I.R. Branham, J. F. B. Mays; and became the pastor of the Brownsville Baptist church, which position he held for three years. He has been thrice married; second wife. Mrs. Rebecca Chilton; third, Mrs. Jane Leigh. Elder Bond has ten children living, three by first, one by second and six by the last; all are professors of religion who have arrived at years of. discretion. Brother Bond as judge, wore the *ermine* with great dignity. As a speaker, he is fluent and impressive. His 'moral character is unsurpassed. He has commanding size and fine address. His attainments are of the first order of scholarship; and withal is very modest and unpretending. He was at one time the president of the Tennessee Baptist convention, and elected the president of the Tennessee Baptist convention at its organization.

He is a good parliamentarian and when presiding commands the respect oft all.

### Isham Richard Branham, D.D.
p. 59-61 from Tennessee Baptist Ministers

Elder I. R. Branham was born in Eatonton, Putnam County, Georgia on December 23, 1825.

In regard to his education, he spent three years at Mercer Institute, Penfield, Ga., during the days when the manual labor system was combined with study. It was through the influence of his grandfather, Thomas Cooper (a leading Baptist in Georgia, and a warm friend of Elder Jesse Mercer), that he went to this institution. (His father was a Methodist.)

He subsequently went to Emory College, Ga., where he graduated in 1847. He was married to Miss Julia M. Iverson, daughter of the Hon. Alfred Iverson, in Mt. Zion, Hancock County, Ga., November 2, 1847; a most estimable lady, of highest culture and refinement.

He was baptized in his thirteenth year, at Penfield, by Rev. Adiel Sherwood, D.D. He commenced teaching school in his native town in January 1848. He was subsequently twice connected with the Georgia Female College, the last time as president. He was afterwards president of the Masonic Female College, Lumkin, Ga. He was six years president of the Brownsville Female College, Brownsville, Tennessee. Here about sixty young ladies were graduated under his charge. While at Brownsville, the degree of Doctor of Divinity was bestowed upon him by Union University, Murfreesboro, Tenn. He is now (1876) the president of Marietta Female College, Marietta, Ga.

He was ordained to the work of the gospel ministry at Madison, Ga., in 1866. The presbytery consisted of Elders N. G. Foster, D. E. butler, J. M. Stillwell and J. M. Springer; was pastor of the church in Madison, Ga., about two years. After his removal to Brownsville, Tennessee, he preached one year at the church in Humboldt, and also one year to the church at Brownsville, Tenn., and part of two years to the church at Stanton, Tenn. He has been the pastor of the church in Marietta, Ga., since July 1874.

As a teacher and trainer of young ladies, Dr. Branham has but few equals and no superiors. It seems that he is exactly fitted to the work, naturally and classically, and having disciplining powers in a high degree. He has the happy faculty of governing by love. The young ladies who were educated by him at Brownsville, Tenn., say they love him next to their father and their mother. The writer remembers upon one occasion being present on a Friday afternoon, being the time of the week's review. He noticed a young lady change her seat during the time; and to show, or give some little idea of his prudent management, he said nothing when the change was made. Being though with the examination the young ladies all acquitting themselves very handsomely indeed, and about to dismiss, Prof. Branham complimented them on their proficiency and in regard to their deportment, remarked that that had been good, with one exception, and he was confident that would not occur again. The young lady caught the arrow and wept, although he made no specification. He rules and governs emphatically by love, causing his pupils to have the highest possible respect for him and his authority. As a minister he was regarded in Tennessee as ranking with the very best in the state. He never attempted to preach without preparation, which was thorough. He thought it an act of the highest presumption for a man to attempt to preach unprepared. His address, enunciation and gestures were all of the most classical sort. While in Brownsville, he was frequently called upon to preach in the city of Memphis, always giving the highest satisfaction to the audience. During his vacations he was not idle, but attended protracted meetings at various points as opportunities provided. He accomplished much and lasting good in this way.

Elder Branham is of medium size, of handsome symmetry; rather deaf; of elegant, courtly manners; of dignified mien; of the highest moral type—cannot bear coarseness nor obscenity; nothing suits him but the haste and refined. As a Christian he is pious; as a minister zealous and of the liberal order; too full of the "milk of human kindness" to make a good "Land marker!" His labors as a Minster have been much hampered and trammeled by the labors of the schoolroom. He can come as near combining the two as any other man, however. He is companionable and social in his bearing and very hospitable. While e is genial and convivial, at the same time he is modest, never thrusting himself forward nor "pulling wires" to gain notoriety or high places. He will live long in the hears of West Tennessee Baptists, and be regarded as one of their noblest brethren.

# WILLIAM SHELTON, D. D.

A pleasant rural home, situated in Smith County, Tenn., was the birthplace of William Shelton. The house in which he was born is still standing. .It is an old-fashioned country dwelling, such as was built by the ancestors of the present generation. His parents were natives of Virginia. They migrated to Tennessee in 1841, and settled in Smith county on the farm where they continued to reside the remainder of their lives.

William Shelton was born on July 4, 1824. In his youth he attended the common schools in the vicinity of his home, alternating study at school with work on the farm until he acquired the rudiments of a common school education. In the fourteenth year of his age he entered a high school then taught at Big Springs, Wilson County, Tenn., where he took his first steps in the knowledge of Latin, Greek and mathematics. In his seventeenth year he entered the junior class of the university of Nashville. While a student at that institution he made a profession of religion and joined the First Baptist church in Nashville, and was baptized by Reverend R. B. C. Howell, D. D., then pastor of the church, and was afterwards licensed to preach. in 1843 he graduated from the university of Nashville in the nineteenth year of 'his age. As there were at that time no Baptist theological institutions in the South, in 1844 he went to New York, and became a student in the Theological Department of Madison university; he giaduated from tbat institution in 1846.

Immediately after his graduation he was called to the pastoral care of the Baptist church in Clarksville, Tenn. Having accepted the call, he was soon afterward ordained to the work of the gospel ministry. The presbytery participating in the work of his ordination consisted of Reverends R. B. C. Howell, D. D.. Samuel Baker, D. D., Reuben Ross, Robt. Williams and R. W. Nixon.

In 1849 he was united in marriage to Miss Virginia Campbell, of Abingdon, Va., a woman of great intelligence, refinement and devotion.

In 1850 he resigned the pastoral care of the Baptist church in Clarksville and accepted the professorship of Greek and Theology in Union university, at Murfreesboro, Tenn. Later, he also accepted the pastoral care of the Baptist church in Murfreesboro, thus doing the double work of pastor - and teacher at the same time. He continued in this position till 1855, when he was offered the presidency of Brownsville Female college, and was called to the pastorate of the Baptist church in that place. Having accepted the position, he removed with his family to Brownsville and entered upon the work before him.

At the opening of the civil war in 1861, most of the students of the college, coming from a distance, were compelled in consequence of the war, to return to their homes, and it was found impossible, amid the exciting scenes, to carry on the regular classes of the college; hence, he used the college buildings, during the continuance of the war, in carrying on a private school, principally for the benefit of the citizens of Brownsville and vicinity.

Immediately after the close of the war, he was elected president of West Tennessee College, at Jackson. Having accepted the position and removed with his family to that city; he succeeded, during the four following years, in building up that institution to a very high degree of efficiency and success. But he had the misfortune, during the spring of 1867, of losing his wife, who was snatched from his embrace by the hand of death.

In 1869 he resigned the presidency of West Tennessee college, and in the autumn of the same year, was married a second time, to Mrs. Caroline W. Bass, of Nashville, Tenn. In 1873 he became financial agent and professor elect of moral and intellectual philosophy in the University of Nashville.

At the organization of the Southern Baptist university in 1876, he was elected its first president. As usual, he became deeply involved in his work, and would have been glad to have remained in the field, but the war came on and frustrated their work, and the missionary spirit has not been revived in this part of the land since. In 1868 he married Miss R.J. Walker, and accepted the call to the care of a little church in Decatur community, which church he served sixteen years; during this time the Lord several times visited the church in the plenitude of His mercy. He had had the care of from two to three churches nearly every year since the war, but he must confess he has not filled the sacred office, serving to provide for himself and family by his own labor. He has been a Landmarker from the first, in faith and practice, and embraces heartily every article set forth in our articles of faith. (Christian, 1926)

## THOMAS OWEN.*

Elder Thomas Owen, of Haywood County, Tenn., was born September to, 1792, in Henrico county, Va. He was the tenth child of Matthew Hobson Owen and Judith Parsons, his wife. Losing his father early in life, it was to the wise, firm and judicious training of his excellent mother, that he owed the impress of his pure, moral character, and his firm and unwavering religious faith in after life. At the age of seventeen, he taught school to obtain means to complete his education. A few years later he took up his residence in Richmond, in the office of clerk of court, where he labored assiduously for several years, in the duties of assistant; in the mean time prosecuting the study of law, to the practice of which he had determined to devote his life. It was during his sojourn in Richmond that the theatre was burned, in which the Governor of Virginia, and so many of her first citizens lost their lives, and but for the firm adherence of Elder Owen to a code of laws which he had established for himself he would have gone to the theatre that evening at the earnest solicitation of a friend, and probably met the sad fate that so suddenly overtook many of his friends and acquaintances. He had made it a rule never to attend the theatre but twice in a season, and he had already attended twice. This firm and unyielding adherence to the rules of conduct, both in morals and in regard to health and exercise of mind and body, was characteristic of him through life, and to this habit he was greatly indebted for his remarkably robust health and activity, far beyond the average of men of his advanced age.

In 1824 Elder Owen embraced religion and joined the Baptist church in his native State. In 1831 he removed to Haywood county, Tenn., and settled near Brownsville, where he spent the remainder of his life. He was one of the original members of the Russell Springs Baptist church; afterwards the Brownsville Baptist church, and he aided much, perhaps more than any other, in shaping the faith and practice of that church. He was ordained in **1831.**

Elder Owen, when not engaged in preaching, spent his time in the study of the Bible and in writing essays on the cardinal doctrines of our holy religion, which are remarkable for the clear and forcible manner in which the various subjects treated by him are elucidated. As an instance, the writer will ever remember his explanation of the doctrine of God's election. "We are the elect," said he, "because we are in Christ, and not in Christ because we are the elect."

He married, a second time, Caroline M. Spivey, who survives him and with whom he-lived nearly thirty-one years In love and happiness. He was kind and affectionate in all the relations of life; a model husband and father. He was for more than half a century a close student of the holy Bible. He seemed to be on most intimate terms with his Heavenly Father, whose word he has loved to study, and consequently his faith was strong and unwavering, and afflictions and misfortunes never weighed him down. He felt and often said, "I am in the hands of a Heavenly Father, who is too wise to err and too good to be unkind." He was perfectly resigned to all the dispensations of Providence; his hope was an anchor of his soul, both sure and steadfast. His last days were peaceful and happy, so loving, so gentle, so softened, so subdued and so cheerful. It seemed that every passion was conquered, and that nothing filled his soul and mind and heart but love to God and good will to man, even to those who had injured and mistreated him. As the physical man gave way, after he had attained his fourscore years, the spiritual man developed more and more, and became brighter and brighter. Never a shadow of a doubt crossed his mind of his final acceptance. He died at his home, surrounded by his loving wife and children and friends, July, 1878, in the eighty-sixth year of his age. (This summary was from the diary of H. B. Folk, Esq., Brownsville, Tenn)

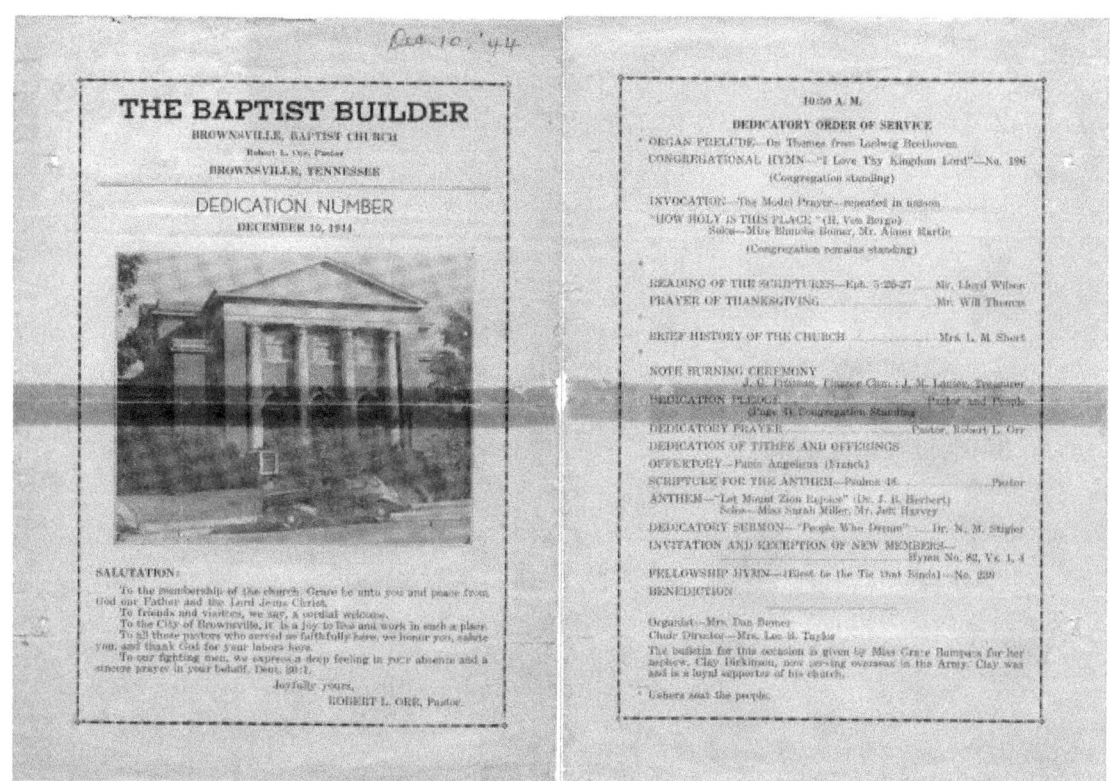

## **Bulletin from Dedication of Sanctuary of Brownsville Baptist Church**

On December 10, 1944, the actual dedication of the long awaited and desired auditorium for the Brownsville Baptist Church was almost a year after its completion. Speakers at this event were former pastors of the church and music was designed to indicate the air of holiness held by the membership for a very hard earned award.

**Members of Congregation in 1930 at Groundbreaking**

Pictured Above:

1. J. T. Davis
2. Carey Lay
3. J. W. McClesh, Mayor
4. Albert Moore
5. W. W. Woodcock
6. S. J. Thomas
7. R. M. Chambliss
8. Albert Thomas
9. J. G. Pittman
10. W. T. Keathley
11. S. J. Turner
12. Dr. W. B. Moore
13. Ben F. Clark
14. Miss Sallie Bond
15. Mrs. L. M. Short
16. Mrs. Thomas

Unknown ladies assumed to be wives of listed men

*Mrs. W. R. Miller, WMU President and her family which are some of the oldest surviving members of the church.*

Emma Haywood Miller
Cherry Haywood Miller
Eldridge (in mothers lap)
James Franklin Miller
William Roots Miller III
Anderson Piatt Miller
Pictured across bottom:
Clopton Miller
Rivers Anderson Miller
Betty Francis Miller

**At the time of this book preparation, Mr. William Roots Miller III was alive and alert at 102 years old. He was the oldest continuous member of the church's congregation.**

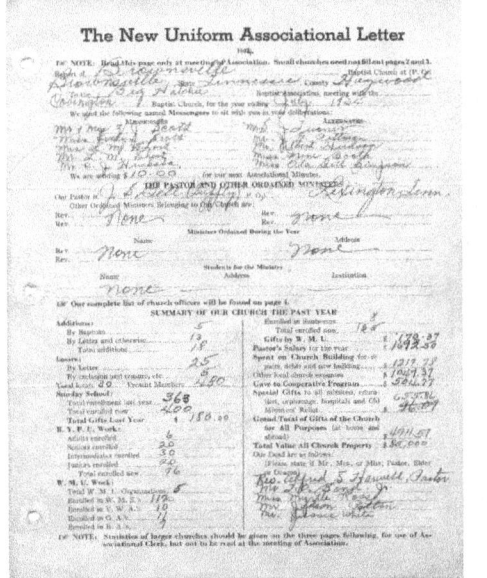
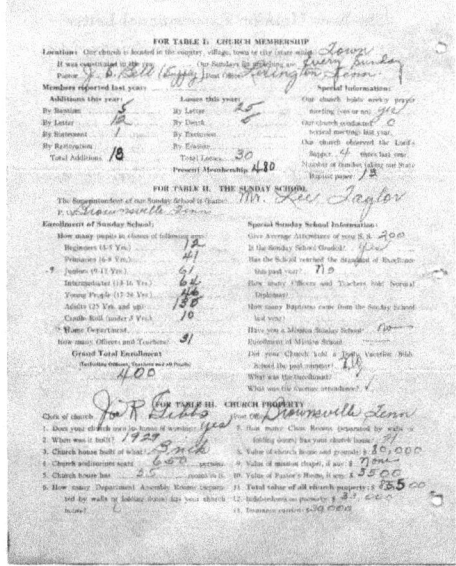

## The New Uniform Association Letter 1914

The church letter submitted to the Big Hatchie Association in 1914, shows some rather interesting figures on attendance and participation. The letter was submitted just after the departure of Bro. Harwell and during the interim of Bro. J.

S. Bell, which of a very short duration. Some of the names found on the document have today relatives, children and grandchildren in the congregation.

## **Men's Bible Class**

*Dr. Sunshine Bible Class (1930's) Front Row: Leslie Shaw, Hascal Hurt, Dr. Fred Roth, Joe R. Gibbs, L. B. Taylor, Roy Moore. Second Row: Unknown, Unknown, Unknown, James Haywood, Marshall Lanier*

The Doc Sunshine Class
1st Row - C. B. Larde, Dick Hawkins, Joe Paehler, Carey Lay, Leslie Shaw
   Hascal Hurt, Rev. Fred Roth (Pastor) J. R. Gibbs, Sr., Lee Bond Taylor,
   Roy Moore, Unknown, Bill Buckler
Identified on second Row and above: Jim Booth, Seymour Haywood, Marshall Lanier, Antonio Sellari, ? Cain, O. U. McKnight, Paul Crider,
Maxwell Bond, ? Binder, Dixie Bond, Al Ferguson, Charles Christmas, C. J. Huckaba, Lloyd Wilson

Men's Bible Class 1953
## The Men's Bible Class

    *Begun in the early years of last century, this group of men began as a gathering of men of different faiths to just study the scriptures together. The date of the organizing is under question as to whether it occurred during the leadership of Judge Bond or under Dr. Fred Roth. At the zenith of the class, it numbered in the hundreds and met at the Court House and eventually in the completed auditorium of Brownsville Baptist Church, which was the only facility at the time large enough to house the class.*

    *Today, the class still meets in Brownsville Baptist Church in the Educational Complex and had twenty to thirty members. Teachers of this class have been Dr. Roth, Mr. Joe Gibbs, Mr. Lee B. Taylor, Mr. Ed Thompson, Mr. Robert Barden, Mr. Wiley Harwell and Rev. Ray Dixon.*

## Vacation Bible School 1953

## Doc Sunshine Class 1940's

## Brownsville Female College 1870's

# Men's Bible Class Ed Thompson, Teacher

# Youth Tacky Party 1950's

# Vaughn-Callery Sunday School Class

# WMU Missions Program 1941

**Intermediates Birthday Party**

*Court House in 1889 with BBC on left behind building*

## 1947 Vacation Bible School

# Bibliography

*A Rat's Chance Cartoon*, The Nashville Banner, Nashville Banner Publishing, Nashville, TN

Abernethy, Thomas Perkins. *From Frontier to Plantation in Tennessee*. Chapel Hill: University of North Carolina Press, 1932.

Allison, John. *Dropped Stitches in Tennessee History*. Nashville: Marshall and Bruce Co., 1897.

Arthur, John Preston. *Western North Carolina, a History, 1730-1913*. Raleigh: Edwards and Broughton, 1914.

*Brownsville Creates a Dream.*, The Baptist and Reflector, Southern Baptist Press, Nashville, TN 1930.

Borum, Rev. Joseph H. *Biographical Sketches of Tennessee Baptist Ministers.* Memphis: Rodgers & Co., Publishers, 1880.

Barnes, William Wright. *The Southern Baptist Convention, 1845-1953.* Nashville: Broadman Press, 1954.

Brownsville Haywood County Historical Society. *History of Haywood County Tennessee, 1989.* Walsworth Publishing, Marceline, MO. Don Mills, Inc. Salem WV. 1989.

Burnett, J. J. **Sketches of Tennessee's Pioneer Baptist Preachers,** Nashville, TN: Press of Marshall & Bruce Company, 1919

Carr, John. *Early Times in Middle Tennessee.* Nashville: Published for Elisha Carr, E. Stevenson and F. A. Owen, 1857.

Christian, John T. *The History of the Baptists.* Two vols. Nashville: Sunday School Board of the Southern Baptist Convention, 1926.

*Clarion-Ledger Obituaries*, Jackson Mississippi, March 7, 2012.

Dawson, Joseph Martin. *Baptist and the American Republic.* Nashville: Broadman Press, 1956.

*Deeds Book L*, Haywood County Registrar's Office, Brownsville, TN

*Duplin County Notes and Events*, Duplin County Genealogical Society, Goldsboro, NC.

*Eleventh Annual Session of the Baptist Conference for the Discussion of Current Questions*, Baptist Congress Publishing, New York 1894.

Free, George D. *History of Tennessee.* Revised edition. Nashville: University Press, 1896.

Garrett, Jr., James Leo **(2009)** *Baptist Theology: A Four Century Study*, Mercer University Press, Atlanta

Garrett, Leroy *TheStone-Campbell Movement: The Story of the American Restoration Movement,* College Press, 2002

Goodspeed. *Early History of Tennessee.* Early Haywood County Churches. Nashville: Goodspeed Publishing Co., 1887

Goodspeed. ***History of Tennessee.*** Sixteen vols. Nashville: Goodspeed Publishing Co., 1887.

Hale, Will T. and Dixon L. Merritt. ***A History of Tennessee and Tennesseans.*** Seven vols. New York: Lewis Pub. Co., 1913.

Hamer, Philip M. ***Tennessee A History 1673-1932, Vol II.*** The American Historical Society. New York. 1933.

Hassell, C.B. & Hassell *Sylvester* **History of the Churches of the Kuhukee Association,** Baylor Publishers, Nashville

Haywood, John. ***The Civil and Political History of the State of Tennessee From Its Earliest Settlement to 1796.*** Nashville: Publishing House of the Methodist Episcopal Church, South, 1915.

***History of the Delaware Street Missionary Baptist Church***, http://www.DelawareStMiss.org 2008.

*"Hot Santa Claus Preacher".* The New York Times, December 26, 1909

Irving, Victor. ***The Country Church in the South,*** University of Virginia Press, 1934

Lane, John J. ***History of Education in Texas***, Governrnent Printing Office, 1903, Washington, DC

McGhee, G. R. ***History of Tennessee, 1663-1930.*** Revised and enlarged by C. J. Williams. Cincinnati and New York: American Book Co., 1930.

***Obituary Dr. E. L. Atwood.,*** St. Petersburg Evening Independent, September 29, 1941

***Oswego Paladium Times***, March 12, 1938

**USGenWeb Rootsweb.com/pub/nc/duplin/cemeteries/laniercem.txt**

**Stott William D.,** ***Indiana Baptist History 1798-1908***, **Franklin College Press, Franklin, IN**

Short, L.M. ***A History of the Brownsville Baptist Church.*** Minutes of the Brownsville Baptist Church, Vol. 2. 1907.

Sweet, William Warren. ***Religion on the American Frontier, The Baptists.*** New York and Cincinnati: Holt, 1924.

**The Booker T. Washington Papers.** The University of Illinois Press. 1982 p 243-245

**The Brownsville Democrat** *"Local Briefs"* Wednesday, March 31, 1875

**The Commercial Appeal**, September 8, 1952. Scripps-Howard Publications. Memphis, TN

**The Martin Democrat**, March 31 1904, Martin Texas

**The Militia of North Carolina 1812-1814,** published under the declaration of the General Assembly of January 18871 by Stone and Uzzell, State Printers and Binders 1873.

Thomas, S. J. ***A History of the Brownsville Baptist Church.*** Minutes of the Brownsville Baptist Church, Vol. 2, 1887.

Nunn, Emma and MacKenzie, Melissa. *A History of the Brownsville Baptist Church.*

*History of Haywood County Tennessee 1989*. Brownsville-Haywood County Historical Society, Walsworth Publishing, Marceline, MO. 1989.

Williams, Samuel Cole. *The Beginnings of West Tennessee.* Watauga Press, 1930.

# Pamphlet Bibliography

Several pamphlets have been used in the preparation of this work although they were not specifically cited as sources. They are:

Thomas, T. D., "*History of the Brownsville Baptist Church 1825-1914*", Church letter found in the W.R. Miller Private Collection. 4 pages

MacKenzie, Melissa Taylor & Nunn, Emma. "*History of the Brownsville Baptist Church 1825 – 1949*" Church pamphlet, Brownsville Baptist Church 1949.

Short, L. M. "Short History of Brownsville Baptist Church 1878-1945", Private collection of Marshall Lanier, Church Clerk.

*Minutes of Brownsville Baptist Church, Vol 1*-6

*Church Bulletin dtd November 6, 1988 p.3*

**Publication** of Brownsville Baptist Church on Observance of 150th Anniversary 1975

# Personal Interviews

*The following personalities were interviewed and quoted in sections of this book. They are:*

*Dr. Robert L. Orr*
*Dr. H. K. Sorrell*
*Mr. H. O. Linyard*
*Miss Betty Goff*
*Dr. D. E. Stewart*
*Mrs. Evelyn Walker*
*Mrs. Melissa MacKenzie*
*Some*

*Rev. James F. Yates*
*Mrs. Emma Nunn*
*Mrs. Sue Short*
*Mrs. Emma Ryals*
*Mr. E. D. Thompson*
*Mr. Paul Bauman*
*Mr. Mike Hickman*

*of the pictures used in this book were provided by Mr. Harrell Clement and are used by his personal permission.*

www.ingramcontent.com/pod-product-compliance
Lightning Source LLC
Chambersburg PA
CBHW081354040426
42450CB00016B/3433